More Praise for Second Guessing God

C. S. Lewis once said that a writer shouldn't aim at being original but being honest, because each individual's unique honesty will bring creativity as well. Brian Jones is both. He expresses the heart's disappointment and longing with a directness that somehow always ends up leading us toward God.

—John Ortberg, author of *If You Want to Walk on Water, You've Got to Get Out of the Boat*

Second Guessing God is a truly marvelous book; Jesus shines brightly on every page. It is laden with spiritual depth and much insight, as Brian Jones leads us on a modern pilgrim's journey toward faith in the midst of darkness. This is one of the best reads I've encountered in years.

—Gary Thomas, author of *Sacred Marriage*

Pull a chair by the fire, put your feet up, crack open this book, and see if your soul isn't as warmed by its wisdom and courage as your body is by the coals.

—Leonard Sweet, author of *Summoned to Lead*

Here is a book that takes deep thinking on the crucial issues of life and deals with these issues in ways that everyone can understand. It is a book that will help every reader along the journey of life.

—Dr. Tony Campolo, author of *Speaking My Mind*

Brian Jones has written an excellent and hopeful book about living the real questions of life from God's perspective. It's clear, fresh, and deep to the heart. I predict this book—and the author—will be around for a long time!

—J. Keith Miller, author of *A Hunger for Healing*

Brian Jones has experienced life in the raw, both personally and as a pastor for over twenty years. In *Second Guessing God* he helps us see that for the child of God there is no pain without a divine purpose. God always knows what he is doing. This is a profoundly moving book and should be an encouragement to anyone who is struggling with God in the midst of pain.

—Jerry Bridges, author of *Trusting God: Even When Life Hurts*

With straight-shooting authenticity and a heartwarming vulnerability, Brian Jones has written an encouraging book for every believer who is honest about doubts. Everyone who hungers for a genuine relationship with God will draw closer to him through this terrific resource. Don't miss out on this message.

—Dr. Les Parrott, author of *Shoulda, Coulda, Woulda*

This is a refreshingly honest look at life. It is a real kick to read. As one late-night host used to say, this is stuff that makes you go "Hmmm." You will feel led to take risks—that's a message we can all use!

—Steve Sjogren, author of *Conspiracy of Kindness*

Brian Jones shares his doubts with us and shows us how to wade through the river of doubt and be anchored to the solid Rock when oceans of questions flood our souls.

—Thelma Wells, Women of Faith conference speaker; author of *The Buzz: 7 Scriptures to Energize Your Life*

It's easy to want to question God's amazing plan for our life—reject it, even. Brian Jones tells why that reaction is not only unwise but unnecessary. *Second Guessing God* is a fresh look at an age-old problem through the eyes of a savvy modern-day pilgrim of the faith.

—Dr. Tim Kimmel, author of *Grace-Based Parenting*

When life puts us in the ditch, we need to know that faith really works. Brian Jones reveals his pastor's heart in this book that will help bring biblical perspective to some of life's most disheartening questions. Read it, be encouraged, and hang on!
—Dr. Joseph M. Stowell, author of *The Trouble With Jesus*

All too often we view suffering as defeat—a failure to exercise faith. With wit and sensitivity Brian shows us suffering is not defeat but a tool God sometimes uses to accomplish his transformational purpose in our lives and the lives of others. The ideas in this book are important for every Christian to understand and apply in order to navigate adversity successfully.
—Ted Haggard, New Life Church, Colorado Springs

Second Guessing God provides practical help to take you through difficult times. Brian Jones seems to have a good grasp of the real questions behind the facades we all build up to survive this thing called life. He strips away the trite and replaces it with honest suggestions for the challenges that every Christian faces.
—Dave Stone, Southeast Christian Church, Louisville, Kentucky

Who of us hasn't second-guessed God weekly? This book will be not only of great personal value but it will be a great tool to help pastor and heal the many confused and broken people we encounter in our caring ministry to others.
—Doug Murren, director, Square One Ministries;
author of *Churches That Heal*

If you know a man who needs a book on suffering, this is it.
—David Hansen, author of *The Art of Pastoring*

Brian Jones puts on paper the thoughts you have in the middle of the night. Then with insight and hope, he leads you all the way to morning.
—Paul S. Williams, chairman, Orchard Group, Inc.;
editor-at-large, *Christian Standard*

Second Guessing God

Second Guessing God

hanging on

when you can't

see his plan

BRIAN JONES

Standard
PUBLISHING
Bringing The Word to Life™

Cincinnati, Ohio

Standard Publishing, Cincinnati, Ohio. A division of Standex International Corporation. All rights reserved. No part of this book may be reproduced in any form—except for brief quotations in reviews—without the written permission of the publisher.

Printed in the United States of America
Jacket: The DesignWorks™ Group
Interior design: Scott Ryan
Edited by Diane Stortz

ISBN 0-7847-1841-5

Library of Congress Cataloging-in-Publication Data

Jones, Brian, 1967-
    Second guessing God : hanging on when you can't see his plan / Brian Jones.
        p. cm.
    ISBN 0-7847-1841-5 (pbk.)
    1. Theodicy. 2. Good and evil. I. Title.

BT160.J65 2006
248.8'6--dc22

2005029542

    12 11 10 09 08 07 06   9 8 7 6 5 4 3 2 1

Dedication

for Craig

CONTENTS

1

Distant

Those who believe they believe in God, but without passion in the heart, without anguish of mind, without uncertainty, without doubt, and even at times without despair, believe only in the idea of God, and not in God himself.

—Miguel de Unamuno

The year before I graduated from seminary, I lost my faith in God. That's not a smart thing to do, I'll admit. There's not a big job market out there for pastors who are atheists. But I couldn't help it. Life was becoming too painful. Truth had become too open to interpretation. The Bible seemed too distant and, as a few of my professors gleefully proclaimed, too unreliable. My doubts seemed to climb on top of one another, clamoring for attention. Before I knew what had happened, the new car smell of my faith had worn off, and I found myself fighting to hang on.

For the next six months, I bought every book I could find that claimed to prove the existence of God. Having so many new books was a good thing, because I rarely slept. There were nights I went to bed at midnight and found myself staring at the ceiling six hours later when the alarm went off. After a while I started taking cold medicine or sleeping pills every few days just to get some sleep. (Years later the taste of cherry cough syrup still makes me nauseous.)

I took long hikes in the woods, not to marvel at God's handiwork but to shout into the trees, yelling at God for not making his existence clear to me. Everything I knew to be true, I felt, was slowly slipping away.

I remember talking to anyone who would listen. I desperately pressed people for details, any clues, any shred of evidence for faith, like a parent looking for a missing child. My wife was wonderful to me during this time, yet for all her graciousness, I felt completely alone in my despair. For the first time in my life, I had panic attacks. I became depressed and even struggled a few times with thoughts of suicide.

During that time the rock group R.E.M. released a song titled, ironically, "Losing My Religion." Whenever I was in the car and the song came on the radio, I stared out the window and sang the words as if I had written them myself:

> That's me in the corner
> That's me in the spotlight
> Losing my religion
> Trying to keep up with you
> And I don't know if I can do it
> Oh no I've said too much
> I haven't said enough[2]

One night, in a last-ditch effort to salvage whatever remnant of faith I had left, I called a mentor and professor of mine from college and shared my struggle with him.

I told him, "My faith in God right now is like a walk on the beach. I've taken off my shoes, and as I stand at the water's edge, the tide has started to roll across my feet. It feels wonderful. Up to this point my spiritual journey has been incredible, but in the last six months doubt has begun to paralyze me. It's like when the water goes back out to the ocean. It is washing away the sand underneath me, and my feet keep sinking lower and lower and lower. If this keeps up, there won't be anything left to stand on."

Without hesitation he shot back, "Brian, I have stood where you're standing. I've felt the water cascade across my feet. I know how wonderful that feels. But I've also had the water go back out to sea. I've felt the sand get washed out from underneath my feet."

He paused—I think he heard me crying—before he slowly finished, "Brian, listen to me when I say this. When the last grain of sand is finally gone, you're going to discover that you're standing on a rock."

That one sentence saved me. That one sentence gave me enough spiritual strength to eventually, over time, rediscover hope, which the Bible beautifully calls "an anchor for the soul, firm and secure" (Hebrews 6:19).

But I wonder about you. As I write these words, I can't help but wonder what struggle you're facing. I wonder what caused you to pick up this book.

WHAT MAKES US STRUGGLE?

I've found that when people doubt the existence or goodness of God or his plan for their lives, one of three things has happened.

Disappointment

One thing that causes us to struggle with our faith is a deep inner disappointment with the way life has turned out. We expected so much more and feel cheated. In Thomas Hardy's classic novel *Tess of the d'Urbervilles,* the main character, Tess, is asked:

> "Did you say the stars were worlds, Tess?"
> "Yes."
> "All like ours?"
> "I don't know; but I think so. They sometimes seem to be like the apples on our stubbard-tree. Most of them splendid and sound—a few blighted."
> "Which do we live on—a splendid one or a blighted one?"
> "A blighted one."[3]

For anyone disappointed with how her life has turned out, it's easy to look at the world this way.

I remember sitting in an airport lobby one afternoon waiting for my wife to return from a trip. My oldest daughter, Kelsey, who was fourteen months old at the time, sat bouncing on my knee as we waited. An elderly lady with a thick eastern European accent sat down near us, and she and Kelsey laughed and played peekaboo for a long time.

Later she leaned over and smiled and said, "You good father. You love. You touch. You hug. You play." Then her entire demeanor suddenly changed and she sternly said, "I had no good father. He kick. He hit. He say stupid. I'm seventy-nine years old, and because father—no lucky day whole life! Whole life!" She turned away, clutching her purse like it was a baby and rocking back and forth, mumbling to herself. My eyes welled up as I thought about how long she had been carrying this wound.

A few minutes later my wife walked through the gate, and after we kissed, we put our daughter in her stroller and walked off. As I looked back to say good-bye to the woman, she waved her finger at me and yelled, "Whole life! Whole life!"

Disappointment isn't rare. I'm sure you can quickly count a number of people you know who feel they were dealt a blighted life. For people of faith this presents a serious problem. Christians believe God can change things. When it seems that he is content to stand by and let us live what we consider a mediocre life, we naturally doubt his presence, goodness, or both.

Many disappointed believers, at their lowest moments, can identify with Woody Allen. In the movie *Love and Death*, Allen's character says, "The important thing, I think, is not to be bitter. You know, if it turns out that there is a God, I don't think he is evil. I think that the worst you can say about him is that basically he's an underachiever."[4]

Brokenness

Another thing that causes us to struggle with our faith is the feeling that we have been broken by life. Life hasn't been just unfair; it has been hazardous. For broken people, being a human being is dangerous business.

Recently my middle daughter, Chandler, shared before dinner that the parents of a friend at school were getting a divorce. Before we ate, we prayed that God would work in the lives of this family. We also prayed that Chandler would be an encouraging influence when she had the opportunity. A couple of weeks later, we asked Chandler how her friend was doing. She stared at her plate and said, "Dad, he's cried every day for two weeks."

French writer Anatole France seemed to speak for those run over by the wheels of life when he wrote what has to be the shortest poem in the world. Three words to be exact. "Born. Suffered. Died."[5] This might resonate with you. Perhaps you feel this could have been written about your life. If so, you're not alone.

When I think of broken people, I think of a homeless man who approached me for money on High Street next to the campus of The Ohio State University. Just eighteen, I had heard somewhere that you should never give homeless people money because they might buy alcohol with it. So I said, "How about *I* buy you something?" The man agreed. We walked to a deli where I bought him a sandwich, a bag of chips, and a soda. When we sat down, I grabbed his hand and said, "Let's pray."

When I finished, I looked up and was surprised to see tears streaming down his face. "How did you end up on the streets?" I blurted out. He rattled off the details like bullet points on a resume: "Successful job; came home from work early one day and caught wife in bed with another man; started drinking; liquor consumed me; lost job; eventually lost house; here I am two years later on the street." I could feel my chest tighten as tears streamed down his face. After a moment he turned his head and pointed out the window to the university buildings across the street. "Do you see that place over there?" he said. "I graduated from that place with honors."

For the next two hours, I shared with him the story of Jesus and how much God loved him. Not surprisingly, he fought off my words like a foot soldier in combat. When we are broken by life, words like "God's love" and "He cares for you" ring like cruel promises in our ears.

Devastation

Finally, many of us struggle with our faith because we have been devastated by life. Life hasn't simply disappointed us or hurt us; it has crushed us. In *Hamlet*, Shakespeare wrote, "When sorrows come—they come not single spies—but in battalions."[6] Maybe this has been your experience, and you have the battle scars to prove it.

A few years ago I organized a support group for women who had been sexually abused. Over the span of two months, I lost count of the number of women who cleared their throats, choked off tears, and said, "What I'm about to tell you, I've never told anyone." The pain these women carried I could actually feel in my body, the whole crushing weight of it. Their despair was insufferable. Many said they didn't believe in God because of what he had allowed to happen, and honestly, I couldn't blame them. I don't know that I could have believed in God either if what they shared had happened to me.

What seemed to hurt these women more than their memories was the despair and utter despondency they felt. It lurked like a stalker in the shadows of their daily routines, following them wherever they went, never leaving their side. When they went to the grocery store, it was there. When they ate dinner, it was there.

When they tucked their kids in at night, it waited in the hallway. It was all they had ever known. Like so many who have been devastated by tragedy or loss, these women had forgotten what life was like before darkness kicked the door down and moved in. Despair had become their new normal.

Disappointment, brokenness, and devastation can cause any of us to doubt the presence or goodness of God and his plan for our lives. But there's hope:

No matter what you've gone through.

No matter how distant God feels.

No matter how confused or numb or cynical or enraged you are.

No matter how much you feel like giving up.

No matter how much you feel like the ground beneath your feet is being swept away and everything you've known to be true is failing you.

In spite of all of this, I promise you can count on one thing: *when the last grain of sand is finally gone, you're going to discover that you're standing on a rock.*

MASTERPIECES IN PROGRESS

Throughout this book we'll explore how the difficult things we experience in life, big and small, are not random freak accidents or streaks of bad luck. They are allowed—and at times even orchestrated—to shape us into the image of Jesus. When tough things happen, especially tragic events, our tendency is to quickly ask, "Why did God allow this to happen?" Instead, the question I want us to begin to ask is, "What is God doing through this difficult circumstance?"

Picture a large rock in the middle of a barren field. Sitting there by itself, it is ordinary, overlooked, and without much use. But in the hands of a master sculptor, it can become a masterpiece. Your life is a lot like that rock.

Even though you can't see it right now, God has been busy creating something breathtaking in you. He has. Through everything you've endured. Through that confusing situation you're facing right now. The problem is we can't see what he's doing while it's happening. All we see are the chips flying. The chisel's blow isn't evidence that God has left us or is angry with us, but rather that God is right in front of us: eyeing our progress, smoothing the rough edges, patiently bringing the image of Jesus out in us.

I need to clarify: when I refer to difficult times, I'm not referring to the consequences of bad decisions *we* have made. Often we want to blame God for allowing consequences to happen.

I remember visiting a man in the hospital. His liver was failing, and he was about to die. He had been an alcoholic his entire adult life, and now that he was dying, he had begun to blame God for his condition. On one visit I couldn't stand his ranting any longer, so I stood up in the hospital room and yelled, "You know what? I've been coming here every day for two weeks, listening to you moan about how God did this to you. Well, you know what? You were the one who went to the bar night after night for the last thirty-five years. You shoved whiskey, vodka, and beer down your throat, not God! So give me a break and quit your whining. God didn't do this to you. You did this to yourself."

Actually, I didn't say that. I was too chicken. But the thought did cross my mind.

I believe God takes even our bad decisions and works to help us overcome their negative consequences. Thank goodness. I've done things unbecoming of a Christian, let alone a pastor, things that would have shocked my friend in the hospital. And those actions have created painful consequences in my life. But I don't usually blame God for those consequences. Deep down inside I know *I* did those things. In my experience, what usually causes people to struggle with their faith is the kind of events the Bible discusses in James 1:2-4:

> Consider it pure joy, . . . whenever you face trials of many kinds, because you know that the testing of your faith develops perseverance. Perseverance must finish its work so that you may be mature and complete, not lacking anything.

"Trials of many kinds." That's specifically what we're talking about. Events allowed or orchestrated by God. That's what God uses to shape us into the image of Jesus. In fact, James says, those things "complete" us.

Now James says something else in those verses that, at first glance, seems quite odd. He tells us to consider such trials "pure joy." Does that sound unrealistic or awkward to you? It does to me. I can think of a lot of things that bring me pure joy, and "trials of many kinds" don't make the list.

Peanut butter milkshakes. Pure joy.

Fishing for rainbow trout on a mountain stream. Pure joy.

Hitting a golf ball three hundred yards. Pure joy.

Playing soccer with my kids in the backyard. Pure joy.

My wife picking out a Victoria's Secret outfit. *Definitely* pure joy.

Finding out my father has kidney cancer. Definitely *not* pure joy.

Why do we react so negatively to God's strategy of using trials to help "complete" us in our spiritual lives? Why is this idea so foreign to us? Most of the time, it has to do with conflicting agendas.

OUR AGENDA

In 1902 William James published his landmark book *The Varieties of Religious Experience.* It was the first exhaustive study ever performed on the psychology of religious behavior. His goal was simple: to share what he thought were the inner psychological motivations for why religious people act the way they do. In that study James observed:

> If we were to ask the question: "What is human life's chief concern?" one of the answers we should receive would be: "It is happiness." How to gain, how to keep, how to recover happiness, is in fact for most men at all times the secret motive of all they do, and of all they are willing to endure.

Later in the passage he concluded:

> With such relations between religion and happiness, it is perhaps not surprising that men come to regard the happiness which a religious belief affords as a proof of its truth. If a creed makes a man feel happy, he almost inevitably adopts it.[7]

That's the root issue. I don't understand the "trials of many kinds" agenda because I have a different one: I want to be happy. It's that simple. And pain doesn't make me happy. Trials hurt. Trials outstay their welcome. I want to be happy today, right now, this minute.

What I want to do is to live in Lake Wobegon, the mythical town created by radio personality Garrison Keillor. In Lake Wobegon, as Keillor puts it, "The women are strong and the men are good-looking, and the children all above average."[8] That's where I want to live. The sun always shines, people always get raises, and when people want to lose weight they go to bed and the pounds fall off. But more importantly, I want God to help pack the moving truck and pay the closing costs to get me there. When he declines, I'm confused.

William James was correct. Happiness was one of my secret motivations for becoming a Christian. I thought that when I became a Christian, God would make me happy, if not all the time at least most of the time. When that hasn't happened, and when tough times inevitably have come, I have found myself questioning my decision to become a Christian, God's existence, or his plan for my life.

The reality is that God knows that happiness, like Lake Wobegon, doesn't last for more than an hour, and then it's gone like a mist. "Happiness" comes from the Old English root word *hap,* which meant "luck" or "chance."[9] Happiness is a fleeting feeling. It's nice when it happens, but you can't predict it. You can't bank on it. Just when you think you can look forward to it, it sprouts wings and flies away.

GOD'S AGENDA

God's agenda is much deeper. God is interested in transformation. God is interested in deep, lasting, and profound change in our lives. This kind of change rarely comes from spending our lives chasing happiness the way a child chases a butterfly. Breathtaking transformation comes through trials. Not one trial, but various trials. Trials of many kinds.

Near the end of his life, Christian journalist Malcolm Muggeridge underscored this when he said:

> Contrary to what might be expected, I look back on experiences that at the time seemed especially desolating and painful with particular satisfaction. Indeed, I can say with complete truthfulness that everything I have learned in my seventy-five years in this world, everything that has truly enhanced and enlightened my existence, has been through affliction and not through happiness.[10]

That's God's agenda.

WHAT'S AHEAD

I want to invite you to go on a journey with me as we discover together this beautiful but often mysterious plan God has for our lives. But before we head out, I want to make a few remarks about the road ahead.

First, I need to communicate up front that this is not an

academic or philosophical treatise. I'm sure trained theologians will read my words and find them wanting. I beg their forgiveness, but I did not write this book for them. My aim is the broken heart. This book was written by, for, and in the midst of people with bruised souls. My goal has been to write a book that one Christian friend gives to another who has seen better days.

Also (I'm sure you can tell by now, but it bears repeating), I'm not an objective observer when it comes to being blindsided by life. I think that's important for you to know. In my journey those who have comforted me the least have always been those who knew all the right answers but had never been through what Spanish mystic St. John of the Cross calls "the dark night of the soul."

Last, I want to clarify what lies at the heart of this book. Ultimately, even though we're discussing why God allows people to go through difficult times, that's not what this book is about. This book is about *recovering joy.* It is about believing again, from the heart and not just from the mind. It is about rediscovering the warmth of God's presence and the conviction that he really does have a plan for our lives.

A few years ago our church was experiencing a growth spurt, and our leadership wanted a better handle on who was attending, why they were coming, and how we could better serve them. So in the middle of our worship service one Sunday, we asked everyone to fill out an anonymous five-question survey.

Later that week I blocked out a few hours in my schedule, sat down with the stack of surveys in my hand, and one by one I read the responses. One caught my attention more than any other.

One of the survey questions was, "What brought you to our church?"

This individual had given a one-word answer:
HOPE.
That's what this book is about.
Let's head out.

NOTES

[1]Miguel de Unamuno, quoted in Madeleine L'Engle, *Walking on Water: Reflections on Faith and Art* (Colorado Springs: Waterbrook Press, 2004), 28.

[2]R.E.M., "Losing My Religion," *Out of Time* (Warner Brothers, 1991).

[3]Thomas Hardy, *Tess of the d'Urbervilles* (New York: Bantam Books, 1891, reprinted 2004), 25-26.

[4]Woody Allen, *Love and Death,* written and directed by Woody Allen (United Artists, 1975).

[5]Anatole France, quoted in H. Wheeler Robinson, *Suffering: Human and Divine* (New York: Macmillan, 1939), 103.

[6]Shakespeare, *Hamlet,* in *The Complete Works of William Shakespeare, The Cambridge Text* (London: Cambridge University Press, 1980), act 4, scene 5, 910.

[7]William James, *The Varieties of Religious Experience: A Study in Human Nature* (New York: Routledge, 2002), 66.

[8]Garrison Keillor, *In Search of Lake Wobegon* (New York: Penguin Books, 2001), 12.

[9]*Webster's New Universal Unabridged Dictionary* (New York: Simon & Schuster, 1983), 824.

[10]Malcolm Muggeridge, *A Twentieth Century Testimony* (Nashville: Thomas Nelson, 1978).

2

Upstream

You will lead me by the right road, though I may know nothing about it. Therefore I will trust you always though I may seem to be lost and in the shadow of death. I will not fear, for you are ever with me, and you will never leave me to face my perils alone.

—Thomas Merton

A few years ago I attended a conference with a friend who is also a pastor. Since we're both pretty cheap, we decided to drive together to the airport and share the cost of gas and parking. Once the conference was over, we flew back, spent an hour trying to find his car in the discount parking lot, stopped at a fast-food restaurant, and headed home.

We were exhausted, but the atmosphere in the van was upbeat. We were excited about what we had just learned, Jimmy

Buffet was playing on the radio, and I had a chicken sandwich in one hand, french fries in the other, and a soft drink wedged between my knees. It was one of those ideal, peaceful moments you always forget about the day after they occur.

As we drove along I-70, outside of Richmond, Indiana, the mood dramatically changed. Without warning my friend suddenly swerved his van hard to the right and almost lost control. Something was in the middle of the road, but we couldn't tell what it was. The car behind us barely missed it as well.

"What was that?" I yelled.

"I don't know. Maybe a deer."

I turned around and was shocked to see a human being standing in the middle of the highway.

"It's a woman! She's trying to kill herself! Pull over!" I pushed the door open and ran to where the woman was standing. By this time she was in the middle of the inside lane, facing oncoming traffic. I edged my way out to her like a police officer inching his way toward someone getting ready to jump off a skyscraper.

"You don't have to do this!" I shouted. "Give me your hand. I'm a pastor. Please. I can help you. Don't do this!" I glanced to my left and saw an eighteen-wheeler coming straight toward her. At the last second she lunged toward the truck, but the driver miraculously missed her. The truck's horn was deafening. I could see the driver scream and arch his back as he struggled to control his steering wheel. I heard the cargo slide and hit the wall of the trailer. Seconds later a van and another truck blared their horns as they drove by, just feet behind me.

Finally, as if receiving a signal from a mother ship somewhere, the woman turned, walked right past me, got into her car, started her engine, and drove off. My friend quickly wrote down her license plate number and called the police, while I stood beside him on the side of the road, shaking and completely unnerved. The rest of the way home we sat in awkward silence, replaying in our minds what we had just experienced.

Through the years I've thought a lot about that woman and what drove her to take such drastic steps. Was she on drugs? Had she committed some unspeakable crime and couldn't shake the guilt? Or did she have a deep wound from some dark place in the past that became too difficult to carry any longer? The question I most ask, however, is what was she thinking? What thoughts were racing through her mind? The whole time I was with her, she never said a word. Not one. But I did get a good look at her eyes. And I've seen that look more times than I can count—hollow, resolute, time for tears long past. Her lips never moved, but her eyes spoke volumes. I'm not a mind reader, but I'd bet anything that I can guess what she was thinking.

She wanted to know: *where's God?*

THE QUESTION EVERYONE'S ASKING

It's a question that graces the headlines of major world newspapers. It comes up on talk shows. Kids wonder about it. Universities create courses to discuss it. It's the question everyone asks when the storms of life hit. Perhaps the most interesting thing about this question, however, is that people ask it regardless of where they are in their spiritual walk.

Spiritual skeptics ask this question. Elton John recorded a song that asks, "If there's a God in heaven, what's he waiting for?"[2] In the past few years, I've listened to the difficult stories of hundreds of spiritual skeptics. Based on what I've heard, I believe the song asks a fair question. When I first became a pastor, I thought that those who opposed the idea of God were just being stubborn. Now I humbly tell people that I've never met an atheist who didn't have a good reason for being one.

Spiritual inquirers ask the question too. Every year I teach a sermon series called "Questions I Want to Ask God." To prepare, I give everyone an index card and ask them to tell me, "If you could ask God only one question and you knew he would give you an answer, what would you ask?" After the cards are collected, I pick four of the questions and try to answer them over the next four weeks. People tell me they love the series because I'm answering their questions. Yet one of the biggest challenges I have doing this year after year is keeping the material fresh. It's no exaggeration to say that almost half the cards, every year, ask the same question in some form: *where's God?*

Many assume that after you've followed Jesus for a long time, you're somehow exempt from ever thinking dark thoughts about God. Unfortunately, you aren't. Even seasoned believers ask the question. When C. S. Lewis lost his wife, Joy, to cancer, he wrote in his journal:

> Meanwhile, where is God? This is one of the most disquieting symptoms. When you are happy, so happy that you have no sense of needing Him, so happy that you are tempted to feel His claims upon you as an interruption, if you remember yourself and turn to Him with gratitude and praise, you will be—or so it feels—welcomed with open arms. But go to Him when your need is desperate, when all other help is vain, and what do you find? A door slammed in your face, and a sound of bolting and double

bolting on the inside. After that, silence. You may as well turn away. The longer you wait, the more emphatic the silence will become.[3]

Everyone asks the question. I guess you're asking it as well. So let me take my best shot at providing an answer.

WHERE'S GOD?

The Bible tells us that for over four hundred years God's people were slaves in Egypt, until God raised up Moses to lead them out of bondage. After their miraculous escape, God did not instruct the people to build a city immediately outside the borders of Egypt. Instead, he told them to follow as he led them to the land he had promised centuries ago to their forefather Abraham, a place of abundance, flowing with milk and honey.

Because of their disobedience, however, a journey that should have taken a month or so eventually took forty years. Now those who were children when they escaped Egypt stood with *their* children and viewed the promised land with their own eyes. They could hardly contain their excitement. Joshua 3 picks up the story: "Early in the morning Joshua and all the Israelites set out from Shittim and went to the Jordan, where they camped before crossing over" (v. 1).

Picture a massive gathering of people, the kind of assembly you see only at political conventions or rock concerts. Over a million people had waited their entire adult lives for this moment. All that stood between them and their future home was the Jordan River. Imagine the excitement as Joshua gave the people God's instructions about when they were to cross the Jordan into the promised land. "When you see the ark of the covenant of the LORD your God, and the priests, who are Levites, carrying it, you are to move out from your positions and follow it. Then you will know which way to go, since you have never been this way before" (vv. 3, 4).

The Israelites soon discovered that Joshua left out one tiny but important detail in his instructions. Joshua 3:15 tells us that the Jordan is at *flood* stage all during harvest. What time of the year was it? You guessed it—*harvest* season! At any other time of year, God's people could have waded across the Jordan, but not during the floods of the harvest season. The river had turned into a raging deluge.

To realize how frightening it must have appeared, you need to understand the topography of the Jordan River valley. On maps the area looks like a roller coaster. One scholar calls it "the earth's deepest valley."[4] The Jordan River begins at the Sea of Galilee and travels just over sixty miles south, where it empties into the Dead Sea, the lowest place on the planet, thirteen hundred feet below sea level. Most of the year it is a tranquil, meandering river, but during harvest season the rainwater converges in the valley basin, and it becomes a swollen torrent.

FACING THE IMPOSSIBLE

We can only imagine how terrifying the Jordan must have looked to mothers holding the hands of their tiny children or to elderly couples clinging to each other. Those with disabilities, those who were sick or blind must have wiped the mist off their faces with panic. Even the swift and strong among the Israelites must have wondered why God had brought them to this point only to let them die. But the passage continues, "Yet as soon as the priests who carried the ark reached the Jordan and their feet touched the water's edge, the water from upstream stopped flowing. It piled up in a heap a great distance away, at a town called Adam" (vv. 15, 16).

Did you catch that? *As soon as the priests' feet touched the water,* God caused the water to stop flowing. In fact, the Bible later tells us that the water stopped completely, the riverbed dried up, and God's people were able to cross over on dry ground. Where did God stop the flow of water? Did it stop right where the people were standing? Did the Israelites see God at work with their own eyes? No. The water "piled up in a heap a great distance away, at a town called Adam" (v. 16).

Scholars estimate the town of Adam was roughly nineteen miles upstream from where the Israelites stood, far beyond where they could see. It was a miracle, but it was a miracle the people didn't witness with their own eyes. God performed the miracle upstream, out of their sight.

I believe the same situation occurs in our lives today. Here's the powerful truth the children of Israel learned that day: *God is always at work upstream in our lives.*

Where's God? Whenever we face a problem in our lives—sickness, job loss, depression, tragedy, or discouragement—God is at work *upstream* in those situations, beyond our line of sight. The only thing the Israelites could see was the problem right in front of them. They could have concluded that since that raging river was there, God wasn't actively involved in their situation, but they would have been wrong. He was there; they just couldn't see him at work.[5]

GOD IS ALWAYS AT WORK UPSTREAM

When I think of examples of God working upstream, I immediately think of the story of my wife, Lisa, who was given up for adoption at birth. Her adoptive parents were Christians and seemed to have a solid marriage when they adopted her, but over the years they realized that even a child couldn't fix their individual wounds. Their relationship grew apart, and their marriage ended in a tumultuous divorce when Lisa was six years old. From that time on Lisa was raised by her mother alone. Times were tremendously difficult for both of them, but they were involved in a loving church that supported them through it all.

Soon after we were married, Lisa expressed interest in finding her biological parents. We couldn't locate them then, but ten years later we resumed the search with the help of the Internet and located both her birth mother and father within one week. To add to the excitement, Lisa learned that she had four half brothers and sisters. Within one month she drove or flew to meet them all.

One of Lisa's half brothers described at length the odd, destructive behavior Lisa's birth mother had engaged in throughout her life. "You're the lucky one," he said. "You escaped." When Lisa heard the whole story, she realized that this was true; she really was the lucky one. Even though, growing up, her life was hard at times, the difficulties were nothing compared to what she would have experienced if her birth mother had kept her. In addition, Lisa's adoptive mother and the church Lisa attended with her had a profound spiritual impact on Lisa's life. This never would have occurred had she stayed with her birth mother. Best of all, Lisa has been given an opportunity to reach out to her newfound family members with the love of Jesus. She hopes now to be a part of what God is doing upstream in *their* lives.

PROVIDENCE

Theologians have a term for God working upstream. They call it the providence of God. Biblical scholar G. W. Bromiley defines *providence* as "the divine governance whereby all possible events are woven into a coherent pattern and all possible developments are shaped to accomplish the divinely instituted goal."[6]

The key part of the word *providence* is the verb *provide*. God is always working behind the scenes in the events of our lives to provide us with something. This is exactly what the apostle Paul said in Romans 8:28: "And we know that in all things God works for the good of those who love him, who have been called according to his purpose."

Notice two things in this verse. First, God works in *all* things; second, he is always working upstream *for our good.* Nothing ever happens to us that doesn't ultimately accomplish God's goals for our lives. God's providence means he is always working behind the scenes, outside of our view, to provide us with *something,* even when we don't understand what's happening at the time.

At the church I serve, I've taught about God working upstream many times, and over the years it has become a mantra among the people in the congregation. I hear it repeated all the time. Something happens to someone—a bad report from the doctor, a child going through hard times, relationship difficulties—and I'll overhear someone else say, "Let me pray for you. God is working upstream in your life right now. Let's pray that he gives you the strength to hold on until you find out what he's doing."

One powerful example of this happened in the life of a dear saint I know named Ruth Ann. (A number of years ago, I attended a Greek Orthodox festival and toured the congregation's beautiful church building. Pointing out the murals on the walls, the tour guide remarked that her pastor once said the reason the Greek Orthodox church has saints is that "saints make it a little bit easier to believe in God." That phrase moved me so much I almost joined their church right on the spot!)

One day Ruth Ann, who was in her late sixties at the time, came down with pneumonia. At two in the morning, she called the ambulance. Ruth Ann was a tough gal, leathered by a hard life, so it didn't surprise me to learn she had asked the paramedics not to use their sirens because she didn't want to wake up her son! The following day I went to see Ruth Ann in the hospital and sat down next to her bed. She was asleep and had an oxygen mask on her face. I reached out and held her hand. She slowly opened her eyes and smiled underneath the mask. I softly said, "You sleep. I'm just here to pray."

A few minutes later Ruth Ann lifted up her mask, just enough so I could hear her whisper, "I know why I'm here. I know why God allowed me to have pneumonia. My nurse is a single mother. She's going through a tough time. I prayed with her last night."

That's God working upstream. More importantly, that's an example of someone who knows the God who is working upstream.

LEARNING TO "SEE" GOD UPSTREAM

How do people like Ruth Ann and like the Israelites crossing the Jordan have so much faith? How do they, in the face of overwhelming circumstances, have within them a sense of peace that God has not left them but is working upstream in their lives? It's because they have learned three difficult lessons that have changed their whole spiritual outlook. The good news is we can learn these same lessons too. The bad news is that there's no guarantee we *will* learn them. The only people who learn these lessons are those who are willing to break deeply ingrained habits and begin to distrust everything they've believed to be true about the world before they became Christians. Let's look at the three lessons.

Trust What You Can't See

The entire foundation of modern science is built upon what we can experience through our five senses—what we can see, taste, touch, smell, and hear. Because of this, many scientists (and people who trust a purely scientific interpretation of the world) only trust what they can pick up with their hands, see under a microscope, reproduce in an experiment, or test with chemicals. Any interpretation of the world beyond this, many scientists say, is pure conjecture.

The problem is that God exists outside our five senses. Unless God chooses to reveal himself in some way, we don't see, taste, touch, smell, or hear him. But that doesn't mean there isn't a God. People who see God at work upstream are those who have learned to look at the world counterintuitively. They've learned to trust what the Bible calls "the eyes of [the] heart" (Ephesians 1:18)—a built-in spiritual sonar in our souls that tells us there's more than we can see.

I, for one, have good reason to distrust what I *can* see. I misread things in the natural world all the time. Recently I was playing soccer at a school playground with my youngest daughter, Camryn, when a couple of screaming four-year-olds joined us. Out of the corner of my eye, I noticed an old, bearded, dirty, eerie-looking man staring at the children.

Of course, I was alarmed. I knew for sure what I was looking at: a bona fide pedophile. I knew I had to do something immediately and was confident that once I acted quickly and bravely, I would be interviewed on television and by the *Philadelphia Inquirer.* The next day people would pat me on the back and say, "Good job, Brian. Did you really wrestle him to the ground and pulverize him single-handedly?"

Confident of my assessment of the situation, I moved in. I walked up to the "predator," looked him squarely in the eye, and asked in the roughest voice I could muster, "DO YOU HAVE KIDS HERE?"

Startled, the man shot back, "Yeah. My grandkids are playing with your daughter." Instantly humbled, I tripped over my words as I replied, "Well, um, of course they are. I just wanted to, uh, introduce myself."

I've learned not to trust what I see. And call me cynical, but I've lived long enough now to watch the scientific community stick to their beliefs like thirteen-year-olds stick to clothing trends. I don't trust what they see either. Do you want to know what I've learned to trust? I trust *the eyes of my heart.* I've learned to trust that part of me that measures beauty and love and passion and truth, all the things that can't be placed under a microscope. This part of me is certain, with every ounce of conviction it can muster, that we're not alone here.

The Bible calls this conviction faith. Hebrews 11:1 tells us that faith "is being sure of what we hope for and certain of what we do not see." The more we exercise faith—trusting God with our souls and not our eyes, our hearts and not our hands—and open ourselves up to the possibility that we can't see and understand everything, the more we'll begin to recognize God working upstream in our lives.

Let Go of What You Can't Control

In *The Great Gatsby,* F. Scott Fitzgerald describes the character Nick Carraway as someone who "wanted the world to be in uniform and at a sort of moral attention forever."[7] Trying to operate the world as Nick did only works if you are a librarian—demanding that people stand in certain lines, living life by unmovable due dates, having everyone and everything in your life stacked neatly and under your thumb. This doesn't work real well, however, if you want to follow Jesus.

Jesus doesn't work on our timetables. He doesn't check with us before he makes decisions. Following Jesus is more like driving a taxicab than being a librarian—you never know who you'll meet or where you'll go next. Following Jesus means giving up control. It means pulling your life over to the side of the road, tossing your keys to Jesus, hopping into the passenger's seat, and saying, "You take it from here."

This is the only way you're going to see God at work upstream, because God can't work in a situation until we get out of the way. As long as we continue to meddle with a problem and try to fix it ourselves, we haven't turned it over to God so *he* can work on it. The Israelites were able to see God at work upstream because they didn't form a bridge-building committee.

Last summer our family vacationed in southeastern Colorado. One bright afternoon my wife said, "Let's go white-water rafting!" Now, if you haven't guessed by now, I might as well tell you: I'm a chicken . . . one hundred percent wimp. White-water rafting is not on my list of the top ten things I want to do before I die. My family was set on the excursion, however, so I reluctantly agreed to go. At the river we joined our group, and our guides put us in wet suits and gave us instructions for the trip. "This is a class III river. You need to know what to do when you fall out of the boat." I raised one eyebrow and turned around and stared at my wife.

Once on board I nonchalantly asked our guide, a left-over hippie from the sixties, if anyone had ever fallen out of one of his rafts. "Sure," he quickly replied, "I lost a group of Japanese tourists a while back. They were fine, though. I picked them up about a mile down river, a little disoriented. You'll be fine today. No worries."

Wonderful. For the next fifteen minutes, I was a wreck. Not my five-year-old. Not my nine-year-old. Not my eleven-year-old. Not my sadistic wife. Just me, a wreck. Then something happened. With each wave I enjoyed the ride a little bit more. I began to pay attention to the scenery: steep canyon walls, layers of deep red rock, and beautiful species of birds I had never seen before. By the end of the trip, I was giving high fives and hollering like a college student at a football game. "I *told* you this would be awesome," I said to my wife triumphantly.

Do you know what's interesting? Not once did I ever lean over to our guide and say, "I'll take over from here." Why? Because I knew the most experienced person in that raft was calling the shots. As a result I could rest and enjoy the ride. It was bumpy. I was scared to death at first, but the ride was much easier than if I had been the captain. The old bumper sticker "Let go and let God" might sound cliché and cheesy, but the saying is true. Some people can't see God at work upstream in their lives, not because they lack faith but because they insist on having too much control.

See Your Pain Within the Bigger Picture

Finally, the last reason we can't see God at work upstream is because we're too focused on today. We become impatient because we want our situation changed right now. We want a miracle—if not today, definitely this week. We'll wait, but it better not take a month!

The Bible is clear about this: God often does his best work over long periods of time. In fact, the Bible portrays God as one who often does his best work over a few generations, not a few hours. That's probably why throughout the first part of the Bible, as if to drive home this point early, God is often referred to as "the God of Abraham, Isaac, and Jacob."

The book of Acts, for example, tells us the history of the birth and growth of the early church. It covers a span of more than thirty years. You would think that what was going on in those days was so important that God would be passing out miracles like a politician handing out campaign flyers. But he didn't. What strikes me as I peruse Acts is not how many miracle stories I read, but how few.

Waiting on God's timing can be frustrating, especially when we're in the hospital lobby wondering about a loved one in surgery or we're thumbing through the want ads. But God can see the big picture; therefore, he isn't as concerned as we are with the short-term fix. Once we learn to accept this, we can develop a mystical kind of patience that asserts, "I can't understand why this is happening, but I'm sure there's a reason for it. I may find out tomorrow. I may find out twenty-five years from now. Or I may not find out until I die. But one day this will all make sense. Until it does, I'm going to relax and give this problem to God."

This lesson became clear one day during my senior year of college when two friends went with their parents on a trip to the Middle East. I was a little jealous. Lisa and I were married and finishing school full-time. We couldn't afford a trip to the gas station, let alone travel abroad. I'll never forget the day our friends got back. We lived on the same floor, so as I heard them coming up the stairs, I went out and welcomed them home.

"Hey," they asked, "could you help us carry something we bought while we were over there?" I agreed, secretly hoping it was a gift for me. It wasn't. It was a large, heavy, foul-smelling rug.

I helped carry it into the apartment and set it down. "Man, we stole this carpet for only a few hundred dollars."

Stole? I thought. *That's the ugliest carpet I've ever seen! I wouldn't have paid ten dollars for that thing!* It looked worn and discolored, with strings hanging out the back.

"It's upside down," our friend said. "Let's turn it over." As he flipped the rug over, I was amazed. It was a genuine Persian rug. The rich colors, patterns, and texture were beyond anything I had ever seen before. I had to take back what I thought earlier—this was a true treasure.

I don't know what you're going through right now, but may I remind you of something? If you're a follower of Jesus, one day your life will end, and God will welcome you into his presence forever. When that happens, I think God will take each of us to the side and say, "Let me show you something. Do you see the back side of this carpet? That was your life on earth. Do you remember when you lost your child? Do you remember when your parents divorced? Do you remember those feelings of depression? Do you remember how awful it was to have your leg amputated?"

Then I think he'll look at you, smile as wide as the sunrise, flip that carpet over, and say, "This is what I was doing through you. Look at the big picture. Look at all the people who were changed because of what you went through. Thank you for being patient. Thank you for enduring the pain. Thank you for being faithful. Thank you for not giving up when you had every reason to do so. This is what I was doing *upstream* in your life."

NOTES

[1]Thomas Merton, *Thoughts in Solitude* (New York: Farrar, Straus and Giroux, 1958), 79.

[2]Elton John, Davey Johnstone, and Bernie Taupin, "If There's a God in Heaven (What's He Waiting For?)," *Blue Moves* (MCA, 1976).

[3]C. S. Lewis, *A Grief Observed* (New York: HarperCollins, 1994), 21-22.

[4]E. G. Kraeling, quoted in Marten H. Woudstra, *The Book of Joshua: The New International Commentary on the Old Testament* (Grand Rapids: Eerdmans, 1981), 58.

[5]I would like to thank my friend, pastor Rick Stedman, for first showing me the power of this passage many years ago.

[6]G. W. Bromiley, *The International Standard Bible Encyclopedia* (Grand Rapids: Eerdmans, 1988), vol. 3, 1020.

[7]F. Scott Fitzgerald, *The Great Gatsby* (New York: Scribner, 2004), 2.

3

Power

*To be a witness does not consist in engaging propaganda,
nor even in stirring people up, but in being a living mystery.
It means to live in such a way that one's life would not make
sense if God did not exist.*

—Cardinal Emmanuel Suhard

My "claim to fame" is that I've been hit on the head by a
television evangelist—twice. Had someone told me six months
before this occurred that I would be on stage with a TV preacher
who was wearing a fifteen-hundred dollar suit and a pinky ring, I
would have said he was insane. I've learned, however, that when
God enters your life, a lot can happen in six months.

I attended church with my parents as a child. I enjoyed the
people there, but I never made the connection between what I
was taught at church and everyday life until I met a guy my age

named Deron. Deron had a way of explaining the key concepts of the Christian faith so that I could understand them. Over four years time I grew to love the God that Deron loved, and after graduation it somehow "clicked" for me. On July 1, 1985, I made Jesus the leader and forgiver of my life.

I dove into spiritual matters head first. Within months I had led a few dozen people to faith in Jesus, started a Bible study at a friend's house, began actively ministering to the poor, and gave up my college baseball scholarship so I could enroll in a Christian college to study to be a pastor. My spiritual fervency at the time was in overdrive.

One night at Bible study, some friends mentioned that a well-known television evangelist was going to be at their church and that I should go so I could receive the "baptism of the Holy Spirit," which, they explained, would enable me to have supernatural experiences like those we read about in the Bible. To which I replied, "Dude, sign me up."

That night there wasn't a vacant seat in the entire church. Dancing in the aisles, arms swaying back and forth, people shouting—it was a sight to behold and reminded me of a college football game, minus the beer and tailgate parties. After the hour-plus-long sermon, the preacher asked people who wanted to receive "the gift" to come up on stage. I assumed "the gift" was what my friends had brought me there for because they all looked at me and nodded.

"There's no way I'm going up there!" I whispered. "You didn't mention anything about going up on stage! I thought there was going to be a class afterwards!" But my friends nudged me into the aisle and the next thing I knew, I was standing up front on the stage with eight complete strangers.

The preacher walked back and forth and yelled into his microphone, "I'm going to need your help, people! Stretch out your hands toward these brothers and sisters!" All over the room people closed their eyes, began praying out loud, and stretched their hands toward the stage as though they were trying to shake hands with the president. Just about the time I was wondering what in the world I was doing there, the preacher began hitting each of the people onstage on the forehead. One by one people fell backward and landed on the ground. When he hit me, however, I just stood there. I felt nothing, but I wondered if I were supposed to fall down anyway. Slightly stunned, the preacher looked out to the crowd and shouted, "Come on, people! Stretch out your hands to this young man!"

The audience roared as people shouted prayers to the stage and stretched out their hands. The preacher turned back to me, took a deep breath, stared into my eyes, raised his right arm high in the air, and yelled "Receive the gift!" as he slapped me on the head again. I didn't fall down this time either. I couldn't believe it. People in the congregation were staring at me as though I were a heathen or an axe murderer. My friends all had an "Oh-my-gosh-will-you-just-fall-down-and-get-it-over-with" look written across their faces. Unsure of what to do, after a few awkward moments I did what any normal eighteen-year-old would have done. I leaned over to the preacher and said, "You're freaking me out" and walked off the stage.

I wasn't sure what to think as I sat in the parking lot waiting for my friends. Even though the evangelist appeared to be a nut case, my friends who attended that church were authentic. They hadn't encouraged me to go that night just to embarrass me. They genuinely wanted me to experience God in a powerful way, and

I wanted that too. That week I reread the stories of Jesus healing people and of his followers experiencing miraculous answers to their prayers. Had people back then made up those stories? Did God stop performing miracles at some point? Or, in my case, was God simply opposed to the manipulative tactics of a spiritual game show host? I honestly didn't know what I was looking for that night, but I do know what I took away from the experience: confusion.

You may be confused as well: You've prayed for Jesus to work in a miraculous way in your life, but nothing seems to be happening. God hasn't brought you that special someone to marry. The cancer isn't gone. You haven't found employment. The relationship you've been praying for still needs mending. You haven't gained clarity about your future. You may be asking why God doesn't work in your life the way he did in the Bible—which is an honest question that deserves an equally honest answer.

WHY DON'T I SEE GOD AT WORK?

In an episode of the television show *The Simpsons,* Bart asks his father, Homer, about his religious affiliation:

> Bart: What religion are you?
> Homer: You know, the one with all the well-meaning rules that don't work out in real life. Uh . . . Christianity.[2]

The show's writers had picked up on one of the key reasons many give up on their faith: they believe it's true; they just don't believe it works. They see a discrepancy between what they read in the Bible and their own personal experience. They read the biblical accounts about the blind who see, the lame who walk, the troubled who find hope, and everybody living happily ever after. But when *they* pray to God, all they hear are crickets chirping in the background. The lame don't leave the rehab center. The blind don't get to watch their children grow up. Nobody they know becomes a Christian and then lives happily ever after.

No wonder renowned atheist Bertrand Russell wrote in the preface of his book *Why I Am Not a Christian,* "The question of the truth of a religion is one thing, but the question of its usefulness is another. I am as firmly convinced that religions do harm as I am that they are untrue."[3] Could that describe how you view your faith right now? If so, let me share two observations that might help put your struggle into perspective.

GAINING PERSPECTIVE

Life Without Miracles

In chapter two I mentioned that God does his best work over long periods of time. That is important to remember. The Bible is a compilation of sixty-six different books written over two thousand years. It just *seems as if* God performed miracles in people's lives all the time because the Bible condenses thousands of years of history into one book. If we don't keep this in mind, we can get a distorted impression of what it was like to live back then. God didn't deliver miracles every day like the morning newspaper. Most followers of God went their whole lives without witnessing one supernatural intervention on the part of heaven.

With some exceptions, the majority of people who lived in biblical times experienced life just as we experience it today.

Two Kinds of Miracles

Another important thing to keep in mind is that the Bible seems to show us that there are *two* different kinds of miracles, not just one.

Instantaneous miracles. The first kind of miracle is the kind we've been discussing so far. It's the kind of miracle where God supernaturally removes or resolves a problem, like when someone is physically ill and God removes the sickness. I call these "instantaneous miracles" because they happen in a moment's notice. The apostle Paul performed instantaneous miracles. "God did extraordinary miracles through Paul" (Acts 19:11). These miracles were immediate. Presto, chango—it's done. Cancer's gone. Sight's restored.

I once volunteered to be a fifth- and sixth-grade boys' counselor for a week of church camp. At registration a mother approached me and mentioned that her son suffered from extreme migraines. She handed me his medication and said, "At some point this week he'll suffer an attack. When he does, give him two of these pills and call me; I'll have to pick him up and take him home."

Sure enough, the next day he tugged on my arm and said, "It's time." I walked him to our dorm, and as I was taking the lid off the bottle, I said, "This may sound crazy, but can I pray for you?"

"I guess," he said.

I gently placed my hand on his shoulder and prayed for Jesus to take the migraine completely away. When I finished, the boy looked up at me and said, "What did you do? It's gone!"

I said, "I think Jesus just took it away."

That's an instantaneous miracle. They're amazing when they happen, but it's important to remember they were extremely rare in biblical times and are just as rare today. In twenty years as a pastor, I can remember witnessing only four such miracles.

Perseverance miracles. The second kind of miracle is the kind where God chooses not to supernaturally remove or resolve a problem. Instead, God gives his ongoing, miraculous strength to us to enable us to persevere through the problem. This kind of miracle happened routinely in the Bible and it still happens as frequently today. I call these "perseverance miracles" because the "miracle" does not occur instantly. James 1:3 tells us that "the testing of [our] faith develops perseverance." The Greek word for perseverance is *hypoméno*.[4] It's formed by the combination of two Greek words: *hypo,* under, and *meno,* to remain. To persevere means to stand up under a heavy trial, the way a bodybuilder lifts three hundred pounds over his head and stands up under it—arms shaking, knees ready to buckle, shoulders splitting with pain—without dropping the weights.

There were times in the Bible when God chose not to instantaneously heal people. Paul ends one of his letters by saying, "I left Trophimus sick in Miletus" (2 Timothy 4:20). Sick? Trophimus was Paul's coworker. Doesn't the Bible say God performed "extraordinary miracles" through Paul? Surely God could have healed Trophimus, but he didn't. Instead, God chose to give Trophimus the strength to persevere through his sickness.

When I think of miracles of perseverance, I think of my dad. The same day I was offered a contract to write this book, I found out my dad had kidney cancer. I was struck by the irony of it all.

I e-mailed my editor and said, "I guess we're going to find out if I really believe this stuff after all." As I began to write, I was convinced God was going to instantly heal my father. Everyone in my church was praying. Everyone in his church was praying. All our friends and their churches were praying. A Christian neighbor visited him the day before the surgery and said, "Don't be surprised when the doctors go in there and can't find anything. Our entire church is praying for you."

As it turned out, God had another miracle in mind. Instead of instantly removing my father's cancer, God chose to leave the football-sized tumor in his abdomen until it was removed by the doctors. As I tried to sleep on the hospital lobby couch that night, I was reminded of how often we pray for one miracle but receive a different one.

Paul describes the miracle of perseverance in 2 Corinthians 4:7-11:

> We have this treasure in jars of clay to show that this all-surpassing power is from God and not from us. We are hard pressed on every side, but not crushed; perplexed, but not in despair; persecuted, but not abandoned; struck down, but not destroyed. We always carry around in our body the death of Jesus, so that the life of Jesus may also be revealed in our body. For we who are alive are always being given over to death for Jesus' sake, so that his life may be revealed in our mortal body.

"Jars of clay" is a powerful analogy. At the time Paul wrote this passage, clay pottery, dishes, and cookware were common. Clayware was common because it was so inexpensive to make—

clay from the ground and fire to harden it were all that was needed. "Jars of clay" were also very brittle. Our minds and bodies are a lot like those jars of clay. We're frail. We break. We crack and fall to pieces. Clay pots don't hold up real well under extramarital affairs, depression, and bankruptcy. When we manage to keep our lives intact when they should be scattered across the floor in a million pieces, we—and others—realize that something supernatural is holding us together.

STORIES OF PERSEVERANCE

Soul Survivors

I remember the first day I met Rita. She attended a Bible study I taught every Tuesday morning for senior citizens. It was our custom at the end of class to go around the room, ask for prayer requests, and pray for each other. Every week Rita asked the class to pray for the same thing—that Jesus would give her strength to make it through another week. Her request never changed. By the tears in her eyes each week, we could tell she was carrying a heavy load.

One day after class I asked Rita if she wanted to share her struggle with me. "It's my husband, Bill," she said. "His temper is so volatile. I don't know if I can make it." Rita was a quiet woman, barely five feet tall and ninety pounds soaking wet. Thinking I clearly understood the situation, I became angry. "I'm coming over tomorrow to straighten him out," I said. "Leave this to me."

The next day as I sat down in their living room, Bill cut me off before I could say a word. "I know why you're here," he said.

"Rita told me she shared with you that we're having a rough time. She's an angel. She really is. She's God's gift to me. I know I'm difficult to live with, pastor, but I've walked a dark road." Then he clasped his hands together, leaned forward, and told me a story that made me feel like someone had punched me in the stomach. Bill had fought in World War II and was taken prisoner by the Germans. They shuttled him around to different places, but eventually he landed in a death camp with a name I vaguely remembered from high school history class: Buchenwald.

Life at Buchenwald was horrific. The guards routinely stripped the prisoners and forced them to walk naked through the fields in the middle of winter. They played mind games, lining up the prisoners as if they were going to be shot and then sending them back to their barracks. Prisoners were beaten and tortured relentlessly; most were killed. The bodies of those who were murdered were thrown into pits of lime to decompose.

Bill told me about a comrade of his with a beautiful eagle tattooed on his back. The camp commander's wife admired the tattoo, and one day Bill's friend disappeared. A few months later Bill walked by the commander's house, looked through a window and saw a lampshade decorated with his friend's tattoo. Women in the camp were raped by prison guards and then, months later, the guards would wrap their legs with rope and force the entire camp to watch the women and babies die in labor.

When I met him, Bill had broad shoulders and stood at least six feet four. As he talked, he reached under the coffee table and pulled out a photo album and pointed to a picture of a skeleton on a stretcher. "Do you see that?" he said. "When they liberated the camp, I weighed less than ninety pounds."

Poet Jane Kenyon is the only person who has ever come close

to describing the despair Bill shared with me that day. In her poem "Having it Out with Melancholy," Kenyon writes:

When I was born, you waited
behind a pile of linen in the nursery,
and when we were alone, you lay down
on top of me, pressing
the bile of desolation into every pore.

And from that day on
everything under the sun and moon
made me sad – even the yellow
wooden beads that slid and spun
along a spindle on my crib.

You taught me to exist without gratitude.
You ruined my manners toward God:
"We're here simply to wait for death;
the pleasures of earth are overrated."

I only appeared to belong to my mother,
to live among blocks and cotton undershirts
with snaps; among red tin lunch boxes
and report cards in ugly brown slipcases.
I was already yours – the anti-urge,
the mutilator of souls.[5]

That was Bill's struggle. From the time he got up until the time he went to bed, he battled the "anti-urge." No wonder he had mood swings. How does someone keep from committing suicide after experiences like his? Honestly, I couldn't even talk. I was so overwhelmed with emotion, I literally couldn't speak. I excused myself and went into the bathroom to try to regain my composure. I felt like I was going to vomit. When I came back to the living room, Bill sensed I was struggling; he graciously put his hand on my arm and said, "It's okay. You don't have to say anything. Jesus will get us through this."

I couldn't have been any more awestruck than if I had personally witnessed the Red Sea part before the children of Israel. Bill and Rita's perseverance was miraculous. How could they endure so much and still hang on to life and each other? Their story illustrates that while instantaneous miracles are amazing when they happen, they are not nearly as amazing as miracles of perseverance.

Why? Because God performs instantaneous miracles by himself. They're amazing, but let's face it, he is God—they should be amazing! Perseverance miracles, on the other hand, depend on God *and* human beings to happen. When perseverance miracles occur, the jury is always out on whether someone like Bill or Rita can get up the next morning and say, "I choose life!" Every time that miracle happens, I guarantee it is not because of the multiple antidepressants Bill swallows every morning. They help, I'm sure, but they're not the main reason his clay jar stays intact. Bill and Rita get up every morning and face another day because an "all-surpassing power" sustains them even in their darkest moments.

Married Strangers

Philip was another "jar of clay" I've been privileged to know. Philip was a Frenchman with a taste for old-school style and charm. Always tanned, he wore freshly pressed white shirts with matching white trousers and a dark blue sports jacket with a white handkerchief in the front pocket. Whenever I spoke with Philip, I felt like I had a brush with European royalty. The look, the way he walked, the tightly structured sentences, the smile—it all reminded me of the way C. S. Lewis described his schoolmaster, Oldie, in the book *Surprised by Joy.* Lewis said, "Oldie lived in a solitude of power, like a sea captain in the days of sail."[6]

One warm afternoon I joined Philip as he made his regular afternoon visit to see his wife of forty-seven years, Claire, who had dementia. When we entered Claire's room, I was struck by how cruel it seemed that after nearly five decades together Philip had to reintroduce himself to his wife every time he saw her.

We sat and talked for a while amidst the sanitary smell of the room with the respirator clicking like a snare drum in the background.

Helen Keller, when describing what her life was like before her teacher, Anne Sullivan, came into her world, borrowed the words of the poet Lord Byron:

> It was not night—it was not day,
>
> . . .
>
> But vacancy absorbing space,
> And fixedness, without a place;
> There were no stars—no earth—no time—
> No check—no change—no good—no crime.[7]

I wondered if that was how Claire felt as she stared at the ceiling day after day: "Vacancy absorbing space . . . fixedness, without a place."

Claire had a single oxygen tube running into her nose and held in place by a piece of gauze tape. In the middle of our forced conversation with Claire, the tape fell off. Philip immediately bent over Claire's bed and began pressing the tape back onto her nose. Startled, Claire looked straight into his eyes and shouted, "Who the heck are you?"

I looked at both of them and tried not to react. Part of me wanted to cry. Here was the mother of his children, the person he lived for every day, and she couldn't even recognize him six inches away. Another part of me felt guilty because I wanted to laugh, because when Claire yelled at Philip, she squinted strangely. It was a cruelly humorous moment, but I sat there, arms at my side, polite.

At that moment Philip looked over at me for a few seconds and then winked. I grinned. He chuckled. Claire chuckled. Then I joined in, and for a few moments none of us could hold back the laughter. We howled so loud and so hard that we began to cry. Claire and Philip looked into each other's eyes and roared, and as I watched the two of them together my tears of laughter quickly turned into tears of wonder. I realized I was watching a miracle in progress. I could have been transported back to the time of Jesus and watched him heal a leper, and I wouldn't have been any more astonished. Here was a man whose clay jar should have been shattered into millions of tiny pieces, but instead, somehow, some way, God miraculously held his life together.

One of the reasons I think God performs more perseverance miracles than instantaneous miracles is because their impact is longer. They stretch. Perseverance miracles aren't flash-in-the-pan. When someone perseveres in the midst of unspeakable hardship, her presence and joy leaves no one untouched. It seeps into boardrooms and kitchens, bowling alleys and nursing stations, front porches and bus stops. Being a living miracle has a much more lasting effect over time on everyone you come in contact with than do miracles that come and go like the wind. That's why, I think, if you give God the choice between instantly healing someone or giving him miraculous strength to live with joy, it's clear which one God will choose and why. When you look at it this way, it's a wonder God performs any instantaneous miracles at all.

TO PERSEVERE, FIND A PAUL

When we realize that God wants us to experience a perseverance miracle rather than an instantaneous miracle, it is easy to become bitter, withdrawn, and negative. During those dark times it helps to have someone in your life who has walked in your shoes before. Every Trophimus needs a Paul.

I'm reminded of the story of the little boy who heard thunder in the middle of the night. The boy ran to his parents' room and begged them to let him sleep in their bed. "I'm scared," he told them. "I *have* to sleep with you." His parents leaned over and said, "Go back to your room and remember that Jesus is with you. There's no reason to be scared." To which the boy replied, "I know Jesus is with me, but right now I need somebody with skin on!"

Sometimes we need someone with skin on too. When we read through the letters of Paul in the New Testament, it's easy to gloss over the lists of names at the ends of each book, names like Aristarchus, Tychicus, Sosipater, Timothy, Phoebe, Silas, Lucius, and Jason. We shouldn't. Each name had a face. Each name carried a story. Each name marked a human being who struggled and probably died serving the same Jesus we serve. One of the reasons I think God left these seemingly insignificant endnotes in the Bible was to remind us of the power of seasoned Christian mentors.

Paul poured his life into these men and women. Everything they went through, Paul beat them to the punch. Imprisoned? Been there. Beaten? Paul had the scars on his face. Discouraged? Lonely? Impoverished? Paul had experienced it all. When Paul spoke about suffering and God's presence and the miracle we experience when we persevere, it meant something; it carried weight. Paul's words brought life. His presence brought calm to anxious hearts, and his perseverance made people believe that they could persevere too. Do you have someone like that in your life? If not, don't rest until you find someone. The lessons you'll learn and the strength you'll gain will be crucial to experiencing a miracle of perseverance.

Someone who was Paul to me was a man named Ray. I met him when we lived in Ohio. Ray had just retired as a pastor from an area church and I begged him to come and be on my staff. He was looking forward to retirement, but he and his wonderful wife, Mary Helen, agreed to work on our staff free of charge for one year. I thought the reason God made this happen was so we would have more hands to start the church. Looking back, I think the reason God crossed our paths was to teach me how to pray.

One day Ray and Mary Helen invited our family over for lunch and said, "When we're done, we can pray for the church." Sure enough, after lunch we put a video on for the children and went back to Ray's office to sit in a circle and pray. Five minutes later I lifted my head, thinking we were done, but Ray and Mary Helen continued praying. I couldn't believe it. I put my head back down and prayed some more, picking my head up fifteen minutes later to look at the clock. They were *still* praying. I lowered my head again, but this time as Ray and Mary Helen prayed, I began to lose track of time. The power and urgency of their words gripped me, my heart slowed down, and I became conscious of my breathing. It felt like Jesus was sitting in the empty chair in our circle, nodding every time Ray or Mary Helen asked him to help someone in need. Over an hour later, as if emerging from a restful sleep, we all lifted our heads and sat silently. For the first time I understood what the disciples must have felt when they listened to Jesus pray and why they cried, "Lord, teach us to pray" (Luke 11:1).

A few years after we moved to Philadelphia, we received word that Mary Helen had a stroke that left her partially paralyzed and unable to walk. Ray rebuilt their bathroom and purchased an electric cart so Mary Helen could travel outside. Unfortunately, her condition worsened over the next few years, and complications eventually took Mary Helen's life.

The time I spent with Ray changed my life. Whenever I'm struggling under the heavy weight of a burden, I always think of the last Christmas letter I received from Ray and Mary Helen before she passed away. Ray wrote the entire letter himself, unlike previous years. He mentioned Mary Helen's complications and the things she was unable to do—she wasn't able to garden; she couldn't go on walks with Ray; they couldn't joke and carry on meaningful conversations as they had. Then he wrote something that made me catch my breath: "Even though Mary Helen can't speak anymore, we still pray together every day."

That's perseverance. It's miraculous.

NOTES

[1]Cardinal Emmanuel Suhard, quoted in Madeleine L'Engle, *Walking on Water: Reflections on Faith and Art* (Colorado Springs: Waterbrook Press, 2004), 26.

[2]"Homerpalooza," *The Simpsons,* written by Brent Forrester, directed by Wesley Archer (original airdate May 19, 1996).

[3]Bertrand Russell, *Why I Am Not a Christian* (New York: Simon & Schuster, 1957), vi.

[4]Gerhard Kittel and Gerhard Friedrich, eds., translated by Geoffrey W. Bromiley, *Theological Dictionary of the New Testament, Abridged* (Grand Rapids: Eerdmans, 1985), 581.

[5]Jane Kenyon, "Having it Out with Melancholy" in *Constance: Poems* (St. Paul: Graywolf Press, 1997), 21-22.

[6]C. S. Lewis, *Surprised by Joy* (New York: Harcourt, Inc., 1955), 26.

[7]Lord Byron, quoted in Helen Keller, *The Story of My Life*, edited by James Berger (New York: Random House, 2003), 317-318.

4

....

Compassion

The most beautiful people we have known are those who have known defeat, known suffering, known struggle, known loss, and have found their way out of the depths. These persons have an appreciation, a sensitivity and an understanding of life that fills them with compassion, gentleness, and a deep loving concern. Beautiful people do not just happen.

—Elisabeth Kubler-Ross

The first time I considered quitting as a pastor was the year we moved to Dayton, Ohio, to start a new church. We had difficulty finding a decent facility to meet in, so we settled for the local junior high school's band practice room, which had no air conditioning. After the grand opening our numbers dwindled from two hundred to ninety people so fast I was convinced the church wouldn't survive. Those who stayed weren't all that happy, including me. The church had attracted a couple of angry people who seemed certain that their personal mission in life was to criticize me in order to keep me humble.

Nothing I tried seemed to help the church grow. I became depressed. I experienced severe migraines. I was so miserable that one day while driving home, I hit the steering wheel with my fist and screamed, "Why did you bring me here to let me fail?" I walked in the door at home and told my wife, "I quit."

As I sat in front of the television that night sulking, a news story aired about a low-income housing neighborhood in downtown Dayton called Parkside Homes. Two people had just been shot there, and the reporter described at length how the violence in the complex caused even the Dayton police to be afraid. The residents rightfully feared for their lives. I sat up and thought, *You know what, it appears I'm not too good at starting new churches, but I bet I can help a few people at that place.*

The very next Sunday I announced to our dwindling group that the last Saturday morning of that month we would all go down to Parkside Homes and show God's love by handing out groceries. You could have heard a pin drop. "You're kidding, right?" someone finally said. "Isn't that the place where people are getting killed?"

I said, "Yes, it is, so bring groceries but leave small children at home." Then I delivered a rousing sermon on sacrifice and quoted liberally from *Foxe's Book of Martyrs.*

As moving as the idea of martyrdom must have been, when the last Saturday of the month arrived, only two women, Suzanne and Mary, showed up. That's it. I looked around and said, "Where is everyone?"

They said, "I think we're it." Over the years I've found that every church has a couple of "spiritual green berets" who will do anything if asked—mow the church grass, feed the poor, clean the local nuclear power plant. Suzanne and Mary were our church's green berets. We pooled our food, which filled my van up to the roof, and headed out.

When we drove into the complex, we were greeted by a scene that belonged in some war-torn country. Trash, graffiti, and abandoned cars littered the area. No one was outside, and that made sense to me. We were petrified just driving into the place. I couldn't imagine what it was like to live there.

As we drove to the back of the complex, we noticed a large group of men huddled together. Since we were not very streetwise at the time, I had no idea we were interrupting a drug deal, and I hopped out of the van.

"Shouldn't we just turn around?" Mary asked.

"No. We're fine. Come on."

As soon as we shut the van doors, the men encircled us. A huge guy, about six feet six, pointed to me and said, "Yo, what the $%#@ are you doing here?"

"We're dead," Suzanne whispered.

I stepped forward. "We're from a church and our van is full of groceries. We want to show people God's love in a practical way. Do you know anyone who needs food?" The man walked up to me and, just inches from my face, stared into my eyes. *Yep, I thought, we're dead.* Then, miraculously, he didn't take the gun sticking out of his pocket and shoot us. He turned to the guys surrounding us, snapped his fingers, and said, "Get people out here." The men began banging on doors and shouting, "Get out here right now! These people have got food and want to show you God's love!"

Within minutes the courtyard was filled with women carrying babies and small children without shoes. I'll never forget their smiles. It was as if someone had pulled back the curtain in a dark room and let the sun fill the room with its warmth. Dozens of people swarmed us. Mary and Suzanne looked at me and said, "We don't know what to do!" I told them to give each person a bag of groceries and ask a simple question: "If Jesus were standing right here, and you knew he would give you anything, what would you ask him for?" They fanned out and with their hands on the shoulders of prostitutes, gangbangers, and heroin addicts, they began to pray.

They prayed deep, powerful prayers, the kind of prayers that make heaven sit up and take notice. Unfortunately, the food quickly ran out, except for one bag. I took it to the tall guy who almost killed me and asked, "So, how about you? If Jesus were right here, what would you ask him for?" He hesitated for a moment, and then he covered his face with his hands and said, "Man, pray for a job. I need a job. I gotta get my family out of this place. I gotta get off drugs. I gotta start over."

I hugged him and whispered a prayer in his ear: "Dear Jesus, give my new friend your strength." I promised I'd be back the next month. I kept that promise and continued to return every month until we moved to Philadelphia four years later.

JESUS' STRATEGY

I didn't realize it at the time, but the trials I had been experiencing were intentional. The migraines, the constant malicious attacks, the discouragement—all were a part of Jesus' plan. Jesus had Parkside in mind. Jesus had in mind struggling single parents I hadn't even met yet. People with mental illnesses, those living on disability, and people who had kids with leukemia were on his mind as he allowed me to reach my breaking point.

Jesus knew that even though I was a pastor, I never would have reached out to these people on my own. Most of the time I was too preoccupied with my own life and daily agenda to notice them, and if I did occasionally reach out to people like these, I didn't understand what they were going through. I hadn't a clue what people were feeling outside the four walls of my comfortable life. My attitude toward others before that day in Parkside reminds me of a line in Herman Melville's novel *Moby Dick*. The main character, Ishmael, is forced to share a bunk below deck with a cannibal from the South Seas. Over time Ishmael's revulsion toward the cannibal slowly melts away, and he says, "I'll try a pagan friend, thought I, since Christian kindness has proved but hollow courtesy."[2]

Before my own brokenness, I'm positive that's what people felt when they interacted with me—hollow courtesy. Jesus knew that in order for me to notice people in pain and reach out to them with authenticity, I needed to go through a slow, painful process of transformation. It's the same process he is taking you through. It involves two steps. Let's look at each of them.

Experiencing Brokenness

The first step in Jesus' strategy for helping us extend authentic compassion to others is to allow us to be broken by hardship. This is what happened to me before Parkside. I admit I can't help but be struck by how strange this approach seems to be. Pain doesn't make people become compassionate; it makes people throw things. It makes us yell. Pain makes people become bitter. When trials hit, the last thing I think about is other people. I focus on my pain and my needs and how God has singled me out from the other six billion people on the planet to endure his wrath. I brood and yell and blame and fuss like a yapping lap dog. The last thing I do when I experience hardship, it seems, is become more compassionate. So if trials make me miserable, how can they be used to help me extend compassion to others? In two ways: our brokenness lets us feel what others feel, and it gives us credibility when we reach out to others who are suffering.

Feeling what others feel. This concept is demonstrated well in Thornton Wilder's short play "The Angel That Troubled the Waters," which is based on a tradition described in the Bible in John 5. In the city of Jerusalem was a pool of water known as the Pool of Bethesda. According to the tradition, from time to time an angel came down to stir up the water, and the first person into the pool after each such disturbance would be cured of whatever disease he or she had. Naturally, then, people who were blind, lame, and paralyzed stayed near the pool day and night.

In Wilder's play a group of invalids sit at the water's edge as a physician walks into their midst and waits for an angel to stir the water. The invalids surrounding the pool scream at him to leave, but the physician explains that he struggles with severe depression and needs to be healed as much as any blind or lame person there that day. As they are talking, an angel suddenly appears. The doctor, in good physical health, lunges for the water. The angel, however, refuses to touch the water, preventing the physician from being healed. The physician sees his reluctance and pleads with him:

> Surely, surely, the angels are wise. Surely, O prince, you are not deceived by my apparent wholeness. Your eyes can see the nets in which my wings are caught. . . .

To which the angel replies:

> Without your wound where would your power be? It is your very remorse that makes your low voice tremble into the hearts of men. The very angels themselves cannot persuade the wretched and blundering children on earth as can one human being broken on the wheels of living. In love's service only the wounded soldiers can serve. Draw back.

Heartbroken, the physician steps back and watches the angel stir the water. Within seconds mangled bodies scrape and claw their way to the edge of the pool. A lucky invalid, the first to touch the water, screams for joy as he jumps up completely restored. As he runs around the pool showing everyone that he's been healed, the physician turns to walk away. Out of the corner of his eye, the newly healed man sees the physician leaving the pool. Moved by the doctor's misfortune, he runs up to him and says:

> Come with me . . . an hour only, to my home. My son is lost in dark thoughts. I—I do not understand him, and only you have ever lifted his mood. Only an hour . . . my daughter, since her child has died, sits in the shadow. She will not listen to us.[3]

And the play ends.

There's a reason why, in love's service, only wounded soldiers can serve. They're the only ones who can understand what another broken person is feeling. Those who have been depressed, like that physician in Wilder's play, have tasted the despair, lethargy, and emptiness that depression brings. Those who have been divorced know the feelings of self-doubt and anxiety that follow in its wake. Those who have struggled with an addiction know how feelings of powerlessness and shame battle inside one's gut like two boxers in the ring. There's a reason why we've gone through what we have: our wounds give us power to feel another person's pain.

When I think of enrollment in love's service, I think of the early years of my marriage to my wife, Lisa. The first two years of our marriage were incredibly tough. We were both in school full-time; Lisa worked part-time, and I carried a full-time job and preached at a small church on the weekends. The only time we weren't exhausted was when we were sleeping, and we didn't sleep much. Over time the stress pummeled our relationship, and we began to fight constantly. We stayed together, but only by the power of God and our unwillingness to quit.

One whopper of an argument started as a kind confrontation on Lisa's part about an area of my life I needed to address. I managed to escalate that into a near nuclear meltdown. I said things I knew I'd regret. It was a Saturday night, and Lisa wanted to stay up and resolve the conflict, but I refused. I barked some unkind words, rolled over, and went to sleep.

The next morning as we both got ready for church, Lisa was surprisingly polite and gracious, not mentioning anything about the night before. As I walked out the door, however, she asked what I was preaching about. I shook my head and stormed out, because as luck would have it, I was in the middle of a series on marriage, and my topic that day was conflict resolution. As I walked away, Lisa yelled at my back, "Go get 'em, *Pastor!*"

But as we did the painful work of learning how to communicate with each other and embrace each other's uniqueness, God began, day by day, to work a miracle in our relationship. By year four what had seemed to be a marriage headed straight for the courts, God and a ton of hard work had turned into an incredible source of joy for both of us. Yet those first two years marked us as a couple. We have always had a place in our hearts for couples in pain, and at every church where we've been we have started groups and classes for couples who are traveling the same hard road we traveled.

Our current ministry is in Philadelphia. When we arrived, Lisa and I worked with another couple on staff to start a marriage renewal course for couples. There have been many highlights. One of the couples stood up in front of the group and held up a stack of papers. "These are our unsigned divorce papers," they said. "We came to this class as a last-ditch effort. In the past eight weeks, God has worked a miracle in our marriage." Then they ripped the divorce papers in half in front of the entire class. The room erupted with applause. When I heard that story the next day, I wondered what would have happened if God hadn't allowed us to have such a tough time during the first two years of our marriage. Would we have felt the need to start that class for hurting couples?

In his book *The Wounded Healer,* Henri Nouwen underscores why it is necessary for Jesus to allow his followers to experience hardship and pain:

Who can save a child from a burning house without taking the risk of being hurt by the flames? Who can listen to a story of loneliness and despair without taking the risk of experiencing similar pains in his own heart and even losing his precious peace of mind? In short: Who can take away suffering without entering it?

The great illusion of leadership is to think that man can be led out of the desert by someone who has never been there.[4]

Our brokenness gives us credibility. The other reason God allows us to be broken by trials is to help us gain credibility with other broken people. When our youngest daughter, Camryn, was six weeks old, she came down with what we thought was a severe cold. We took her to the doctor and he told us to take her immediately to the hospital, where she was diagnosed with RSV (respiratory syncytial virus). Doctors told us RSV is easily treatable but that Camryn had such a bad case she needed to be hospitalized.

Later that night as I stood next to the plastic bubble my daughter had been placed in, I asked the respiratory therapist giving her breathing treatments if RSV was deadly. "Tell me the truth," I said.

"Honestly, Camryn's condition is serious," she replied. "About twenty-five hundred children die from this each year. Rather than worrying, though, why don't we let the medicine do its work and let God do the rest?" But for the next two nights, Lisa and I were beside ourselves with worry. I can honestly say I have never prayed as forcibly as I did during those forty-eight hours.

Camryn survived. Soon after her hospitalization I visited

a young mother in our church whose newborn son had been placed in pediatric critical care in a different hospital across town. Doctors believed her son had bacterial meningitis, a disease more threatening than RSV. Watching her baby through the same type of plastic bubble Camryn had been in, the mother asked me, "Have you ever seen this part of the hospital?" I told her that we had been in a pediatric critical care unit not too long before with our own daughter. Then I said, "I believe this is the part of the hospital where God hangs out." She looked at me and nodded, and then we stood there for the longest time without saying another word.

Our own suffering allows us to speak with credibility to other people in pain because we've been in their shoes. We've walked the road they've walked. When we talk, other broken people listen because what we say and what we do carries weight. I'm reminded of the words Rainer Rilke used to conclude a letter he sent to a struggling young poet he had taken under his wing:

> If there is one thing more that I must say to you, it is this: Do not believe that he who seeks to comfort you lives untroubled among the simple and quiet words that sometimes do you good. His life has much difficulty and sadness and remains far behind yours. Were it otherwise he would never have been able to find those words.[5]

That's the first step in Jesus' strategy. Jesus allows us to be broken so we can feel what others feel and so we can have credibility in their eyes. He does not stop with our brokenness, though. Once we are broken, God fills our emptiness with something powerful.

Getting Jesus' Heart for People

The second step in Jesus' strategy for teaching us to extend authentic compassion to others is to give us his heart for the broken people around us. Soon after I came back from that first visit to Parkside, I came across a seemingly insignificant verse in the first chapter of Philippians: "God can testify how I long for all of you with the affection of Christ Jesus" (v. 8).

The book of Philippians is a letter the apostle Paul sent to a congregation he had started less than a year earlier. Since our church in Ohio was also in its first year at the time, I was struck by the similarity between our church and the Philippian congregation. I became intrigued by Paul's statement that he had "the affection of Christ Jesus" for the Philippian people.

I wanted that kind of emotion for the people in my church and community, so I did some further study on the word *affection*. I found that *affection* in that passage comes from the Greek word *splanchna,* which means "guts."[6] Many times it was also translated "compassion." In the Bible *splanchna* is used literally to describe the inner parts of the chest cavity, such as the heart, lungs, and blood vessels, but it is also used figuratively to describe the overwhelming compassion someone feels towards another person in need. When I watch a sad movie, my jaw tightens, my chest constricts, I get a lump in my throat, my eyes water, my heart races. That's *splanchna,* an overwhelming feeling of compassion for another person.

Paul, however, went one step further and said that he had *Jesus'* affection and compassion for people, which led me to look up how the Bible uses *splanchna* in descriptions of the ministry of Jesus. I discovered that Jesus felt *compassion* for just about everyone he met:

"When Jesus landed and saw a large crowd, he had compassion [*splanchna*][7] on them, because they were like sheep without a shepherd" (Mark 6:34).

When Jesus saw a woman who had lost both her husband and only son, "his heart went out to her [*splanchna*] and he said, "Don't cry'" (Luke 7:13).

In the story of the good Samaritan, Jesus said, "But a Samaritan, as he traveled, came where the man was; and when he saw him, he took pity [*splanchna*] on him" (Luke 10:33).

And in probably the most famous example, the story of the prodigal son, Jesus said, "But while he was still a long way off, his father saw him and was filled with compassion [*splanchna*] for him; he ran to his son, threw his arms around him and kissed him" (Luke 15:20).

After I finished reading these verses in the original Greek, I lifted up my head and said out loud, "That's exactly what I was feeling at Parkside Homes." I felt *splanchna* for those people.

This was one of those eureka moments in my spiritual journey. I realized that feeling in my heart wasn't an accident. Something was happening inside me spiritually. I bowed my head and prayed, "Jesus, please give me the same affection for people that you have."

This became my constant prayer. I would talk to someone in the hallway and say to myself, *Jesus, give me your heart for this person.* In fact, I probably prayed that prayer a dozen times a day, and I still do. Whenever I'm with someone in need, I always ask Jesus to give me his compassion for that person. I want to feel what he feels for that person. I want his heart, his emotions, his mind, and his love for everyone I meet.

Whatever circumstances you are facing right now, I want to

encourage you to begin praying that prayer as well. While you are pumping gas, ask Jesus to give you his heart for the person monitoring the pumps. As you're walking by your neighbor's house, pray that Jesus would give you his heart for your neighbor and his kids. Every time you go to church or your child's school or walk into the cafeteria at work, pray for the compassion of Jesus. When you do, two amazing things begin to happen.

Seeing what Jesus sees. The first thing that happens as you pray that prayer is that Jesus allows you to see what he sees when he looks at people. Soon after I began praying this prayer, an elderly man began attending our church. My wife, always the extrovert, invited him to join our family for lunch one Sunday at a Chinese buffet. It was the end of May, so to start the conversation I asked our new friend if he was planning a vacation anywhere over the next few months.

"Yes," he said. "In fact, I'm going to Florida next week."

I knew he was single, so I joked, "I bet you're going down there to find a girlfriend!"

He laughed and described at length the different ocean resorts he planned to visit. At some point he casually mentioned "clothing optional" beaches.

I smiled, waited for him to finish, then slowly put down my fork and asked, "Did you say *clothing optional* beaches? We've been all over Florida and never saw a beach like that." He assured me that they were everywhere and said that he could give us Web addresses for them if we wanted to know more.

Now, I'm not the sharpest person in the world, but after ten minutes of this, I put two and two together and asked, "Are you a nudist?"

He looked at me, tilted his head to the side, smiled, and said, "Yes, I am." (In my mind flashed an image of elderly people playing nude volleyball, and I quickly lost my appetite for sesame chicken.) Then he reached in his back pocket and said, "Let me prove it." He pulled a card out of his wallet and slid it across the table. It was an identification card (my kids were sitting with us so I was glad it wasn't a picture ID!) that read, "American Association for Nude Recreation."

Not knowing what to say, I handed the card to Lisa and remarked, "Well, how about that?"

Lisa grinned and said, "Yep. That proves it all right!"

Realizing that a conversation about what the Bible has to say about nude senior citizens running around on beaches was a subject better suited for another time, we graciously brought our lunch to a close. We paid for our meal and hugged our interesting new friend good-bye. Once inside our van I laughed and said, "I have got to be the only pastor in America with a card-carrying nudist in his church!"

What I remember about that conversation is not so much the details of what this man told us as the way I reacted as he spoke. I felt an incredible sense of compassion. It was as if God allowed me to see past his behavior to the inner wounds that drove the behavior. It seems strange to say this, but as I conversed with him I sensed Jesus' heart beating inside me and reaching out to this man through me. It was as if I could actually see what Jesus saw— a wounded, broken man.

In his book *I and Thou*, philosopher Martin Buber says there are essentially two kinds of relationships in the world.

"I and Thou" relationships—person to person, and "I and It" relationships—person to object.[8]

Having Jesus' heart for people keeps us from turning people in our lives into *it* people. You know what I mean by *it* people. When we treat the bank teller no differently than we would an ATM machine, we have turned him into an it. When the cashier who takes our order at a drive-thru doesn't even have a face, we've turned her into an it. Sometimes we even live in the same house with *it* people.

Jesus never met an *it* person. Jesus noticed everyone. He had an I-Thou relationship with everyone he met. Every interaction he had with another person meant something to Jesus. He didn't eat a meal and then two minutes later forget the name of the person who served him. That's what having Jesus' *splanchna* does to us. It sensitizes us to people and their needs. When we have Jesus' heart, we see what he sees as if we're borrowing his eyes.

Feeling what Jesus feels. The other thing that happens as you pray to have the compassion of Jesus is that he will allow you to feel what *he* feels for people in pain. Frederick Buechner once said, "Compassion is the sometimes fatal capacity for feeling what it's like to live inside somebody else's skin. It is the knowledge that there can never really be any peace and joy for me until there is peace and joy finally for you too."[9] That's what it's like to have Jesus' heart for people.

Soon after I began to ask for the compassion of Jesus, I noticed an imposing stone building that stood a few hundred yards off a major road near where we lived. A sign said "The Stillwater Center." I had driven past the place four or five times a day, and it had never occurred to me to find out what it was. Now I thought it had to be some kind of nursing home, and if so, then maybe our church could reach out to the residents in some way.

I knew that having Jesus' heart is not just about having a warm feeling for people in pain but is designed to prompt us to alleviate whatever pain we encounter. With this in mind, I pulled into the driveway and navigated the winding road that led back to the building.

When I entered the foyer, I introduced myself to the receptionist and inquired as to what service the facility provided. She must have thought I was a reporter doing an investigation, because she quickly said, "Hold on, I'll get the director." A few minutes later a man greeted me, and I told him I was a local pastor and that I had driven past the facility hundreds of times, wanted to know a little more about the center, and wondered if there was any way our church could serve there.

The director seemed hesitant, but he began to explain that the facility cared for people with severe mental retardation and physical challenges. "We take care of people when their parents can't take care of them or they've been abandoned," he said. "The best way to explain what we do is simply to show you." He took me through a long corridor into what looked like a large hospital emergency room. From a distance each bed seemed to hold a large stuffed animal. But walking up to one bed, the director said, "This is Stephen. He's eleven."

Stephen was maybe three feet long and looked like a mound of clumped flesh. He lay there motionless, his arms and fingers curled into a ball. I asked how long Stephen had been at the center.

The director replied, "As long as I can remember." Then he turned to the girl in the next bed. "This is Laura." I looked at Laura but quickly glanced away because she was much more deformed than Stephen. Laura had only part of a face.

The director continued talking, and I couldn't help but notice what he did as he spoke. He took his index finger and slowly parted Laura's hair to the side and tucked it back behind her ear. Then he caressed her deformed cheek. As I watched, I thought, *If Jesus were here, he would have responded just like this man.*

After the tour the director walked me to my car and thanked me for stopping by. He mentioned that he was a Christian and said something about Jesus being the only thing that got him through each day.

As I drove off, I couldn't shake the image of him pushing Laura's hair behind her ear. Some might say he was just born with a naturally compassionate personality, but human compassion would have worn out after two months on that job. He was intelligent and obviously skilled at what he did, but training only takes you so far when it comes to caring for people; after a while everything becomes mechanical. After a moment I realized I didn't have to guess anymore. I knew what fueled that man's compassion. It was his heart or, rather, Jesus' heart. He had Jesus' heart for that little girl.

Either that or perhaps Laura was his daughter.

NOTES

[1] With permission from the author, Elisabeth Kubler-Ross.

[2] Herman Melville, *Moby Dick* (New York: Penguin, 1988), 49.

[3] Thornton Wilder, edited by A. Tappan Wilder, *The Collected Short Plays of Thornton Wilder* (New York: Theater Communications Group, 1998), vol. 2, 74-75.

[4] Henri Nouwen, *The Wounded Healer* (New York: Doubleday, 1990), 72.

[5] Rainer Maria Rilke, translated by M. D. Herter Norton, *Letters to a Young Poet* (New York: W. W. Norton, 1934, reprinted 1993), 72.

[6] Colin Brown, ed., *The New International Dictionary of New Testament Theology* (Grand Rapids: Regency Reference Library, 1986), vol. 2, 599.

[7] Technically, throughout Jesus' interactions with people in the gospels the verb *splanchnizomai* is used instead of the noun *splanchna*. I chose to carry the noun form throughout this chapter for the sake of clarity and brevity.

[8] Martin Buber, translated by Ronald Gregor Smith, *I and Thou* (New York: Charles Scribner's Sons, 1958), 3.

[9] Frederick Buechner, *Wishful Thinking: A Seeker's ABC* (New York: HarperSanFrancisco, 1993), 18.

5

Doubt

It is said that in some countries trees will grow, but will bear no fruit, because there is no winter there.

—John Bunyan

One of the most well-known passages in the Bible is Matthew 28:18-20, referred to by many as the Great Commission because it outlines Jesus' final marching orders for his followers:

> Then Jesus came to them and said, "All authority in heaven and on earth has been given to me. Therefore go and make disciples of all nations, baptizing them in the name of the Father and of the Son and of the Holy Spirit, and teaching them to obey everything I have commanded you. And surely I am with you always, to the very end of the age."

Over the years I've heard more sermons, read more books, listened to more tapes, and had more discussions around that passage than any other in the Bible. That passage was one of the initial reasons I decided to become a pastor. Churches, mission organizations, colleges, and other ministries around the world point to that passage as the basis for their existence: to help every person on the planet become a follower of Jesus. It's undeniable that Matthew 28:18-20 has become the international rallying cry for Christians everywhere.

There's a glitch though: we've distorted the original meaning of the passage. Any student of literature knows that in order to properly understand a passage, you must read it within the context it was originally written. Anyone can lift a passage from just about any text and interpret it to mean whatever they want it to mean. Unfortunately, this is what many Christians have done with Matthew 28:18-20.

Notice how this same passage sounds when I add the two verses that immediately precede the Great Commission. Matthew 28:16-20 (with italics added) reads:

Then the eleven disciples went to Galilee, to the mountain where Jesus had told them to go. When they saw him, they worshiped him; but some doubted. Then Jesus came to them and said, "All authority in heaven and on earth has been given to me. Therefore go and make disciples of all nations, baptizing them in the name of the Father and of the Son and of the Holy Spirit, and teaching them to obey everything I have commanded you. And surely I am with you always, to the very end of the age."

Do you see the difference two verses can make? Notice how even two words—"some doubted"—changed the entire tone of the passage. Who doubted? The context tells us that "the eleven disciples went to Galilee," so "some" refers to a few of the original disciples Jesus gathered and trained. We're not told specifically which ones. All that we're told is that some doubted.

For years I skimmed over those preceding verses (vv. 16, 17). Then one day last year I was studying this passage again while preparing for a sermon, and I was struck by the words "some doubted" as if reading them for the first time.

There is great irony in the way those two verses precede Jesus' Great Commission. Jesus' disciples had just spent three years watching him perform awe-inspiring miracles, not to mention his last and greatest miracle of all—rising from the dead. After that experience, the last people on earth one would ever suspect of doubting are these eleven disciples. Aside from this, it's ironic that Matthew chose to include "some doubted" at all. Couldn't he have left those words out? I'm sure he was tempted to gloss over this seemingly minor incident, but he didn't. Why? I believe he deliberately penned these words because he wanted to communicate a very important truth to all future Christians: struggling with doubt is a natural part of being a follower of Jesus.

Surely Jesus knew what his disciples were thinking. Here stood the very people who were going to take over his worldwide mission, and still doubt lingered in some of their minds. But what did Jesus do? Did he get angry and say, "Guys, I'm furious. This doubt you're experiencing is a show stopper. I'm not sending you anywhere until you wrestle those questions to the ground and reassure me that you're one hundred percent convinced of who

I am and my plan for your lives"? No. Instead, he sent them out *with* their doubts.

Based on the entire context, then, the more accurate message of the Great Commission is that doubt is a natural part of the Christian life and that Jesus uses people who struggle with doubt to change the world.

The reason it is important to acknowledge this is that doubt has a way of bubbling up to the surface when we experience hardship. When I think of doubt, I immediately think of the very first car Lisa and I owned, a 1988 Ford Escort. It wasn't exactly the sleek sports car I had always envisioned as our first automobile, but it worked for us. Even though I had never been much of a mechanic, I was fanatical about that car's maintenance. I always made sure there was gas in the car, and I checked the oil like clock work—whenever the "check engine" light came on.

One day as I was driving, a massive plume of smoke came out the exhaust pipe and consumed the cars behind me. Seeing this, I realized it was probably a good time to check the oil. I pulled the car over, popped the hood, and took the oil cap off. Brownish gunk was caked all over it, which the mechanic informed me later was soot from the engine. Apparently, as oil lubricates an engine, it carries the engine soot back to the oil pan, where it falls to the bottom and settles until guys like me forget to put oil in the car. When that happens, the mechanic said, this sludge gushes to the top of the pan, races back into the engine, and turns to smoke in the exhaust, causing people behind me to choke and swerve into light poles!

Doubt is much like the dirt that settles in the bottom of a car's oil pan. As long as we own the car, it will be there. When things are going great, our lives are like a well-oiled car—

everything is flowing the way it should, and the soot stays at the bottom of our souls. When we face trials, however, our doubts become agitated and rise to the surface. Most of us instinctively assume that doubt is bad and needs to be pushed back down to the bottom of our spiritual oil pans. In fact, this assumption is often reinforced by the Christian subculture. Books, tapes, videos, seminars, and ministries abound to help Christians quickly eliminate their doubts.

In the Great Commission passage, however, we don't find Jesus in such a hurry to do this. It is as if Jesus saw the practical benefits of allowing our doubts to find some fresh air. Describing her own spiritual journey, Madeleine L'Engle wrote, "I had yet to learn the *faithfulness* of doubt. This is often assumed by the judgmental to be faith*less*ness, but it is not; it is a prerequisite for a living faith."[2] I think Jesus felt the same way. What happens when we doubt?

DOUBT KEEPS US HUMBLE

Six months after I graduated from seminary, I wrote a letter to the editor of our local newspaper. A radical group of New Testament scholars, operating under the name The Jesus Seminar, had come to town for one of their annual meetings. Their audaciously self-appointed task, as a group of "biblical experts," was to decide which teachings of Jesus were authentic and which, according to their research, had been fabricated by the early church. I was concerned that their claims might adversely affect people's faith, so I wrote a disparaging letter about their meeting to the editor of our local newspaper. To my surprise my letter was placed at the top of the editorial section. The response it generated was beyond anything I expected.

Dozens of Christians from all over the county tracked me down and sent me notes congratulating me for my boldness. I was swamped by phone calls both at the office and at home. I also received some hate mail, including a quasi death threat. It came sealed in a package with an FBI cover letter that read, "The sender of this letter is under federal investigation. Please alert us of any unusual activity." I thought, *Oh, that's wonderful!* That next Sunday a man came into our worship service with a crowbar and sat near the front. When one of the ushers noticed him sitting in his seat angrily tapping the crowbar onto his palm, he alerted a few off-duty police officers in our congregation, and they forcibly removed him from the church building. I'm sure little kids watched this and thought, *Church is awesome!*

The problem with my letter was that it was only partially accurate. I listed all the reasons why I felt the words of Jesus in the Bible were trustworthy. I conveniently forgot, however, to include that I had lost my faith just a few years earlier and still had lingering doubts that plagued me. I'm sure that because of my lack of humility, my letter appeared condescending to many of the newspaper's readers, including our church's crowbar visitor.

Writer G. K. Chesterton once said that a madman is someone who "is in the clean and well-lit prison of one idea: he is sharpened to one painful point. He is without healthy hesitation and healthy complexity."[3] In my early years I felt my job as a pastor was to defend God. I felt it was my duty to present a nonwavering spiritual front, even if that meant not being completely honest about my own misgivings. I felt it was my job to shove my suspicions deep down inside and lock them in a corner closet of the basement of my soul. This, I was convinced, would inspire people; my certainty would rub off on others and give them certainty as well.

A few years of serving people in churches cured me of that. Helping the chronically unemployed, visiting six-year-olds with leukemia, praying with women who had been raped, and taking groceries to quadriplegics has a way of removing false pretenses. I quickly learned three words that I find myself uttering a lot these days: "I don't know." I don't know why you lost your son. I don't know why God gave you the parents he did. I don't know why a lot of things happen anymore.

Somehow I don't think Jesus envisioned his followers sending patronizing letters to newspaper editors or acting as if they have the answers to all the world's questions. I believe that as Jesus uttered those final words in Matthew 28, he knew that a good dose of occasional doubt would give his followers the healthy hesitation and healthy complexity we all need to stay humble.

THE DISCIPLINE OF DOUBT

The second thing that happens when we doubt is that we are forced to discipline our emotions. One day in college I went to speak with a professor with whom I had a close relationship. "I'm struggling with my faith right now," I said in frustration. I explained that in the last few days everything seemed gray. Questions were plaguing my mind. Life seemed more difficult than usual.

My professor smiled and said, "You and Lisa are having problems, aren't you?"

I was furious and shot back, "Absolutely not. I can't believe that you would assume such a . . . er . . . um, well, maybe. We had a little argument. We've been talking about marriage, and she thinks we should wait until after graduation to get married. But I love her and I don't want to wait." It was clear he knew that what I was really wrestling with was my emotions and not God.

When we are going through tough times, one of the hardest things to discern is whether our doubts stem from a genuine struggle with God or our current emotional state. I amaze myself at how quickly I can go from being on top of the spiritual world into "oh-my-gosh-my-life-is-horrible-and-there-is-no-God" mode. Speaking of this problem C. S. Lewis wrote:

> Now Faith, in the sense in which I am here using the word, is the art of holding onto things your reason has once accepted, in spite of your changing moods. For moods will change, whatever your reason takes. I know that by experience. Now that I am a Christian, I do have moods in which the whole thing looks very improbable: but when I was an atheist, I had moods in which Christianity looked terribly probable. This rebellion of your moods against your real self is going to come anyway. That is why Faith is such a necessary virtue: unless you teach your moods "where they get off," you can never be either a sound Christian or even a sound atheist, but just a creature dithering to and fro, with its beliefs really dependent on the weather and the state of its digestion. Consequently one must train the habit of Faith.[4]

Just like you, there are times I have genuine doubts, but if I'm being honest, there are just as many times I doubt because

I've had too much pizza the night before or simply because I'm exhausted. I've learned, for instance, not to make any major decisions as a pastor on Mondays. After speaking and being with people all day Sunday, I'm emotionally spent come Monday. For years I felt like something was wrong with me every Monday—the world looked bleaker, my passion for spiritual matters bottomed out, and I was more irritable than usual. Some Mondays I would even allow myself to wallow in the depths of despair. It took me quite some time to discipline myself to realize that I couldn't trust what I was feeling on a Monday. If I was feeling the same thing come Tuesday, I would address it then. If not, I knew I could attribute my "Monday morning blues" to emotional exhaustion and leave it at that.

LIVING WITH OUR QUESTIONS

The third thing that happens when we doubt is that we are taught to live with unresolved questions. A few years ago I stumbled across an old purple tub in the corner of my parents' basement. Inside was a collection of keepsakes from my childhood, lovingly saved by my mom years ago. I smiled as I pulled out items I hadn't seen in decades: an old varsity letterman jacket, fifth- and sixth-grade football trophies, faded pictures with crumpled corners.

To my surprise, underneath a tee-ball trophy and a wooden plaque sat a white, spiral-bound book entitled *School Years* that held all my old report cards, kindergarten through twelfth grade. On the back of my very first report card, Mrs. Johnson, my kindergarten teacher, had written, "Brian is progressing well in all of the above areas. However, he is somewhat shy in volunteering and answering questions." Then, under the section marked "Parent Comments," my mom had replied, "We were quite surprised to hear that Brian is shy in volunteering and answering questions. He is basically not a shy child at all. We casually asked him about his responses in class, and his only comment was, 'I'm not shy, Mom! I just don't know all the answers!'"

The funny thing is that after all these years, I *still* don't know all the answers. For instance, one of these days I'm going to write a book called *Passages I'll Never Preach*. In that book I'll include all the parts of the Bible that don't make sense to me. The first chapter of Hosea is one of them. God tells the prophet Hosea to find a prostitute on the streets, take her home, marry her, and have children with her, despite knowing that some of her children will not be his. One of the children Hosea and his new wife, Gomer, have together is a little girl that God tells them to name *Lo-Ruhamah,* which means "not loved." We're told that God wanted the people of Israel to have a visible reminder, as a warning, of the ultimate result of their unfaithfulness to him (v. 6). This passage makes perfect sense—as long as you're not that little girl. I have three daughters and know how words affect their hearts and minds. I can't help but be sickened when I read that story. I can't understand how God could make someone go through her entire life with the name "not loved." Surely God could have come up with another way to communicate his point.

Perhaps you have a question that is bothering you. Maybe something happened to you or someone you love, and there doesn't seem to be any rational explanation for its occurrence. How do we resolve these kinds of questions? Honestly, most times we don't. We live with the ambiguity. We wake up every day knowing full well that we carry around with us just as many questions as answers. I used to purchase every book I could find that attempted to provide factual proof for the truth of the Bible and the Christian faith. After a while, however, I realized that those books helped me very little. This troubled me until I realized that the books are written backwards. These books only present the final product. I want to know how the authors got there. I want to hear about their sleepless nights, agonizing in despair. What I want to read is a book written by someone who is bold enough to list all of his unanswered questions but is still willing to die for his faith.

At the heart of a life filled with unanswered questions lies the very nature of Christianity. Our faith is about a relationship with Jesus, not an adherence to a set of intellectual ideas we can memorize and master. Doubt reminds us of this. In Matthew 28:16-20, the disciples could walk away from that mountain and continue to follow Jesus with all their doubts because they were following *him*—a real, living, breathing person—not a book. Jesus and his disciples were in relationship with each other, and that relationship took precedence over the disciples' need to have all their questions answered.

It's the same with us today. Poet Rainer Rilke could have been writing to us when he counseled:

> I want to beg you, as much as I can, dear sir, to be patient toward all that is unsolved in your heart and to try to love the *questions themselves* like locked rooms and like books that are written in a very foreign tongue. Do not now seek the answers, which cannot be given you because you would not be able to live them. And the point is, to live everything. *Live* the questions now.

Perhaps you will then gradually, without noticing it, live along some distant day into the answer.[5]

EXPERIENCING THE ABSENCE OF GOD

There have been numerous times in my spiritual walk when my soul felt like it was in a lush oasis of God's presence. There have been other times I've been so full of doubts I thought I had wandered off into a spiritual desert and wouldn't be found until days later, face down in the sand, disoriented, and on the verge of spiritual death. During those times I've felt abandoned, confused, angry, and worst of all—without hope.

I think the word *desert* is a perfect description of a Christian's experience of God's absence. When *desert* is used in the New Testament, it is a translation of the Greek word *erĕmos,* which means "solitary" or "abandoned."[6] This is exactly how I feel when I am experiencing intense doubt. I feel abandoned by God, utterly alone. I feel spiritually lethargic, like I'm lying face down in the sand, dehydrated. During these times of doubt, I have no passion left for participating in church, reading the Bible, prayer, or anything related to God. All I feel is emptiness, as if a large presence just left a room.

Yet the Bible attests that sometimes our greatest spiritual transformations occur in the desert. For the children of Israel, their forty-year wandering in the desert changed them as a people. Fasting forty days and nights in the desert at the beginning of his ministry marked Jesus. Galatians 1:17 tells us that after the apostle

Paul was first converted, he immediately went to Arabia. We're not told how long he was there or what he did, but we do know that he came back a changed person. Spending time in a *spiritual* desert can foster some of our greatest moments of spiritual growth.

What specifically does God's absence do in our lives?

Burning Up Bad Spiritual Fuel

One thing God's absence does is "burn up" any remaining bad spiritual fuel that we've been using for our souls. There are two components to bad fuel. The first is our unhealthy motivation for becoming Christians in the first place. It is important to acknowledge that none of us becomes a Christian out of pure, uninhibited love for God. We usually have ulterior motives. Some of mine? I wanted to avoid Hell, I wanted to get fixed emotionally, I wanted to find a Christian wife, and I wanted to please my parents. All of these factors played very heavily into my decision to become a Christian. When difficult times arrived, I discovered these motivations weren't nearly powerful enough to sustain my dedication to Christ. The cost of remaining a Christian outweighed my original motivation for becoming one, and I was faced with a choice: find a new motivation or walk away.

The second component of bad spiritual fuel is living only for the aftereffects of our relationship with God, rather than for God himself. As new Christians we experience a rush of feelings: peace, joy, happiness, warmth, excitement, contentment, and a host of others. Over time we inadvertently become dependent upon these feelings to sustain our spiritual well-being. We begin pursuing the feelings we receive from God rather than pursuing God himself. This is dangerous because, as Simone Weil once remarked, "There is a great danger in loving God as the gambler loves his game."[7] We can become spiritual-experience junkies, pursuing one spiritual fix after another just to get through the day.

What God's absence does is usher us into a state of complete emptiness, where all these feelings are taken away. During these stretches our impure motivations for becoming a Christian no longer sustain us. All feelings of contentment and peace leave us, and we're forced to learn to love God simply for the sake of loving God and not for what we can get from him. It's as if God says to us during these parched moments, "It's easy to love me when you *feel* close to me. How about when my peace and warmth are gone; will you love me then? I'll leave the room for a while, and we'll find out."

Near the end of the sixteenth century, a Spanish monk later known as St. John of the Cross was imprisoned at the age of thirty-five for supporting reforms of the Catholic Church. Fellow monks locked him inside a tiny closet they had used as a bathroom and brought him out only to be flogged in front of the other monks while they ate dinner. He suffered starvation and was not given any extra clothes or blankets during winter or fresh air to breathe during the squelching summer months. Eventually his clothes began to rot on his body. In the depths of his despair, John began composing love poems to God. His guards were so moved by what he shared with them that they began smuggling pen and paper into his closet so he could write.[8]

After nine months, John escaped from his captors. Afterward he put what he learned during that desert period into a book entitled *The Dark Night of the Soul.* Speaking from experience, John described the way God's absence purifies us and enables us to reach deeper levels of spiritual maturity:

> When they [spiritual beginners] are going about their
> spiritual practices with the greatest enthusiasm and pleasure
> and it seems to them that the sun of divine favor is shining
> most brightly upon them, God suddenly darkens all that light.
> He slams the door shut. He cuts off the source of the spiritual
> waters they had been drinking from . . .
>
> Left in such aridity, not only do they find no satisfaction in
> their reliable old spiritual practices, but these things actually
> become tasteless, even bitter.
>
> God sees that these souls have grown a little. He weans
> them from dependency on the breast so that they can become
> strong. He lays aside their baby clothes and sets them down from
> his arms so that they can learn to walk on their own two feet.[9]

St. John's story reminds us that even dark nights eventually give way to the sunrise, but while they are happening those dark periods can be difficult beyond comprehension. We must remind ourselves during these painful moments that just because we can't feel God's presence does not mean he has abandoned us. Sometimes God does his greatest work when we're lost in the desert.

Reaching Out to Others

Probably the most well-known story of someone experiencing God's absence is told in the book of Job. Stripped of everything in life—his health, his family, and his wealth—Job is brought to the point of utter despair. By the end of the book, though, God replaces much of what was taken during his desert experience. However, I'm left with the impression that Job was never the same person after his trials, no matter how wealthy he later became.

I think one of the reasons this book was included in the Bible was to show us that times of doubt and God's absence are meant to be experienced in community with others. The book of Job is forty-two chapters long. Seven of those chapters are devoted to what God did and said, while the remaining thirty-five chapters, roughly eighty percent of the book, are dedicated to the conversations Job had with his three friends Eliphaz, Bildad, and Zophar. I believe one of the lessons God wants us to learn from Job is that navigating spiritual deserts was never meant to be a solo activity.

This past year I went through the third major desert experience of my life. My first desert experience occurred while I was in graduate school, which I described in chapter one. The second was as a young church planter in Dayton, Ohio, which I told about in chapter four. But my third desert experience is recent.

Our church in the suburbs of Philadelphia grew to over eight hundred people in less than four years, and I was exhausted— mentally, emotionally, spiritually. I began questioning whether I was cut out to be the pastor of a large church. The larger the church grew, the more my soul shriveled. The demands placed on me were incredibly toxic. We were adding more staff and buying more land and raising more money than I felt I could keep up with. It seemed so strange that at the same time the church was exploding, my soul was imploding. I began to question why God would "call" me to do something but not give me the necessary gifts to be able to get the job done. I became desperate and anxious. I stopped reading my Bible. I stopped praying. I went through the motions at church, feeling numb to it all. For the second time I seriously contemplated quitting the ministry, and I felt completely alone.

One afternoon I began journaling on my laptop. I typed for hours, pouring my heart out to God. In the middle of those paragraphs, I wrote a poem I called "The Awful Journey":

> Take me to the place where no one else will go
> Take me to the place where despair and hope
>   crash into one another
> Show me the person who knows the awful journey
> Show me the person who knows the dark road
>
> I'm at the ledge and have lost my footing
> The rocks loose underneath my feet
> Holding on to nothing but my will to survive
> I look for another
>
> Show me the person who can stand with me
> Point me to the one who knows many sleepless nights
> Show me that person
> Let me hear you doubt out loud

A few weeks later, out of desperation, I reached out to a mentor of mine in the ministry and shared with him my thoughts from that day, including the poem. I e-mailed him and told him I didn't want to quit being a pastor but wasn't sure I had the strength to go on. I was afraid and alone and didn't know what to do. A day later when I checked my e-mail, I saw his response. The few words at the beginning of his e-mail were exactly what I needed to hear. They reminded me why it's always best to take dangerous trips through the desert with friends at your side:

Brian,

Well, I like the poem.

I'm traveling the same journey. You do know that, right?

I like your description of the awful place.

Of course, it is also an awe full place.

NOTES

[1]John Bunyan, *Advice to Sufferers* (Swengel: Reiner Publications, 1968), 9.

[2]Madeleine L'Engle, *Walking on Water: Reflections on Faith and Art* (Colorado Springs: Waterbrook Press, 2004), 135.

[3]G. K. Chesterton, *Orthodoxy* (New York: Doubleday, 2001), 16-17.

[4]C. S. Lewis, *The Joyful Christian* (New York: Simon & Schuster, 1996), 130.

[5]Rainer Maria Rilke, translated by M. D. Herter Norton, *Letters to a Young Poet* (New York: W. W. Norton, 1934, reprinted 1993), 34-35.

[6]Colin Brown, ed., *The New International Dictionary of New Testament Theology* (Grand Rapids: Regency Reference Library, 1986), vol. 3, 1004.

[7]Simone Weil, translated by Arthur Wills, *Gravity and Grace* (New York: G. P. Putnam's Sons, 1952), 103.

[8]St. John of the Cross, translated by Mirabai Starr, *Dark Night of the Soul* (New York: Penguin Putnam, 2002), 5-6.

[9]Ibid., 59-60.

6

Sight

It is usually in the wake of frustration, in moments of crisis and self-disillusionment, and rarely out of astonishment at man's glorious achievements, that radical reflection comes to pass.

—Abraham Heschl

I have to be the worst fisherman in the world. I began fishing when I was a small kid, so you would think I would be a pro by now, but I'm not. I'm horrible. I couldn't catch fish with dynamite. This being the case, I got excited when we moved from Ohio to the suburbs of Philadelphia to start a new church. I thought that regardless of how the church turned out, I could at least restart my fishing career where no one knew me. You can imagine, then, my disappointment when I realized the new location only brought new problems. People on the East Coast don't fish for catfish and largemouth bass with bobbers and the tools God intended—they fish for trout with fly rods and fancy equipment they sell at preppy, outdoorsy stores. I was in trouble.

You should have seen my first day out on a trout stream. I had all the equipment the slick salesman at the store told me I needed: the special trout net, the tan vest with all the pockets that held my gadgets, the nine-foot fly rod with the weird-green floating fishing line, the waterproof waders that went all the way up to my chest, and a carton of hand-tied artificial trout flies that resembled fuzz pulled off old shirts. I looked like Barney Fife with waders.

I remember the day vividly, not so much because I looked so ridiculous but because of the perfect stranger on the bank of the stream making fun of me. Each time I cast my line into a tree or snagged my vest, he howled with laughter. He even started pointing out my blunders to his friends. The more I cast my line, the more he laughed and the more furious I became. Eventually, I got so angry that I just about waded over to him and snapped his fishing pole in half.

I resisted this urge for two good reasons. First, we were surrounded by a large group of people. Second, he was only six years old.

Just as vivid in my memory, however, is the day, months later, when I actually caught my first trout. I was with a friend who seemed to pull something out of the water with every cast, so I asked him why he thought he was catching fish and I wasn't. After all, I was wearing my special vest and expensive waders and *still* wasn't catching fish; something had to be wrong. He pulled his sunglasses off, handed them to me, and said, "Put these on and look into the water." I walked to the edge of the stream, put his glasses on, and immediately realized why he was catching fish. He could actually see them! With these glasses, I could see all the way to the bottom of the stream, whereas, without them, I could only see the top of the water.

"What are these things?" I asked, dumbfounded. He explained that they were polarized sunglasses designed to shield his eyes from the glare that came off the water. Without the glare, he was able to place the bait right in front of the trout and have a greater chance of catching them. So I wore his sunglasses for a while, and believe it or not, they worked. I caught my first trout, all eight inches of it. I raised my arms in the air and shouted, "I am the man!" as if I had just caught a great white shark.

I think the trials we experience in life are a lot like those sunglasses: they allow us to see things we would never see without them. Novelist Madeleine L'Engle described one of her characters this way: "She had a touch of second sight, that gift which allows us to peek for a moment at the world beyond ordinary space and time."[2] That kind of perspective is a great gift to have, but it doesn't happen on its own. You aren't born with it. It doesn't come as a result of hard work or education. The only situation that comes bearing the gift of second sight is the one we try to avoid at all costs: trials—painful, prolonged, heartbreaking trials. Yet, I believe that if the situation that gives this gift is so painful, then God must know that the reward we receive will be equally incredible. What does God see that we don't? What could be so important, so special, and so life-changing that God allows us to experience heartbreak just to catch a glimpse of it?

WHAT WE GLIMPSE THROUGH SUFFERING

The Culture of Illusionary Prizes

When I was a kid, the city where I lived hosted an annual Easter egg hunt at a park down the street from my house. One year as I stood at the starting line, I spotted, off in the distance, the golden egg. Each year the officials of the event placed one large, glistening golden egg in each age group's section of the hunt. The child who discovered it would triumphantly claim a large prize in front of all the other kids.

This was my year. I, alone, had seen the golden egg, tucked underneath the right-field fence on baseball diamond number four. When the gun went off, I ran with all my might past all the eggs lying in the field, not wanting to pick any up and slow myself down. I blew past my friends Chris and Steve and eventually reached the fence, winded and sweaty. When I bent down to grab my prize, I couldn't believe my eyes: my golden egg had turned into a shiny candy wrapper! All along it had been an illusion. I was crushed. I turned around and looked back across the field. By that time all the other eggs were gone. I walked home that day without a single Easter egg in my basket.

I've heard it said that as we grow older, the games we play don't change, they just become more expensive. I believe that. In our culture people are consumed with finding the golden egg. I know I struggle with this pursuit at times. What's interesting about golden eggs is that they differ for each person. For some of you, your golden egg is your body. You're consumed with looking great and will do anything, pay anything, add anything, and cut anything to get it. For others, your golden egg is money. You're consumed with becoming the next Bill Gates, currently one of the richest men in the world.

For others, the golden egg is stuff—cars, boats, homes, clothes, jewelry, vacations. As I write this chapter, talk show host Oprah Winfrey is busy redesigning a home in Montecito, California, larger than her ninety-seven hundred square foot home in Chicago. Her new fifty-million dollar, twenty-three thousand square foot home is located on forty plus acres complete with an additional guest house, gatehouse, two ponds, and a lake. Maybe that's your golden egg—to live in a home the size of a small eastern European country.

Whatever your golden egg is, God tells us it's an illusion; it isn't real. Not that some people won't find their golden egg eventually. It's just that when they do, it won't deliver the blissful happiness they want it to deliver.

Unfortunately, some people spend their entire lives chasing golden eggs. At the end of Tolstoy's *The Death of Ivan Ilyich,* the main character, Ivan, who has sought power and prestige his whole life, lies in bed in excruciating pain. When his physician arrives, Ilyich refuses any pain medication and throws the doctor out of his room, choosing instead to fully experience his final moments with clarity. Tolstoy observes:

> It was true, as the doctor said, that Ivan Ilyich's physical sufferings were terrible, but worse than the physical sufferings were his mental sufferings, which were his chief torture. His mental sufferings were due to the fact that that night . . . the question suddenly occurred to him: "What if my whole life has really been wrong?"

Then Tolstoy adds:

> It occurred to him that what had appeared perfectly impossible before, namely that he had not spent his life as he should have done, might after all be true.[3]

We read that and we tell ourselves that we would never allow ourselves to be in that position. But we shouldn't be so presumptuous. One Saturday I saw a nature show with a king cobra swaying its head back and forth and staring at a rabbit. The commentator said that the cobra was hypnotizing his prey. As the cobra's head moved back and forth, the rabbit just sat there, motionless and stunned. Then, without warning, the cobra struck with furious speed and killed the rabbit instantly.

That image reminds me of the Bible's warning, "Do not love the world or anything in the world" (1 John 2:15). The Greek word the Bible uses for "world" in this verse is the Greek word *kósmos,* which means either "world" or "beauty," depending on the context.[4] We derive our English word *cosmetics* from it. In the first century *kósmos* was used to describe not only the order of the world but also the beautiful things *in* the world, such as stunning statues, beautiful people, and breathtaking natural wonders. Why, then, does the Bible in this context use *kósmos* negatively?

I think it's because God knew we could easily fall into the hypnotic stare of our culture and waste our lives, just like the rabbit and just like Ivan Ilyich, seeking happiness from what was created rather than its creator. God's gift to us then, in those lethal moments, is to send trials to shake us free from our culture's grasp to see our situation for what it really is. This is crucial, because what writer Simone Weil once said is absolutely true: "If there were no affliction in this world we might think we were in paradise."[5]

When I think of the way this works, I recall an experience Lisa and I had soon after we moved to Dayton to start a church. As our new congregation there began to deteriorate, I became consumed with keeping the thing afloat. I threw myself into the task, working insane hours to make this dream of mine happen. Let me underscore the words *dream of mine*. My life during that period resembled the scene in *Gulliver's Travels* where the six-inch-tall people of the island of Lilliput emptied Gulliver's pockets of its contents. Upon seeing his pocket watch, they proclaimed it must be his god, because "he seldom did any thing without consulting it."[6]

One day, in the middle of this whirlwind, we were driving home from a lunch appointment with a potential staff member. I looked in the rearview mirror and noticed a bump on my one-year-old's neck as she sat asleep in her car seat. I slammed on the brakes in order to assess this bump, which as new parents we immediately assumed was a tumor. Nervously we rushed to the doctor's office for a diagnosis: a swollen lymph node—nothing to be worried about. We sighed a deep breath of relief.

That incident, however, startled me so much that I began regularly checking her for similar bumps, just to be on the safe side. One day, sitting in a restaurant, my finger rolled over a bump just above her left shoulder blade. This time, however, I was relaxed, assuming it was a swollen lymph node, just like before. But we had it checked out, and when the doctor turned to us and said, "I want to take this out," our hearts sank. Later that week, as they rolled my little girl into surgery, it was as if God handed me a special pair of glasses and said, "Here's what's important. Take a look. That golden egg you're chasing, that's an illusion. You think you're doing my work, but you're not. The work I gave you just went in for surgery."

That moment both scared me and changed me. Here I was, presuming to do God's work, when all along I was caught in our culture's spellbinding definition of success and ignoring my family in the process. If it hadn't been for that jolt, I might never have seen my life for how shallow and selfish it had become and changed my behavior. That experience, though I would never want to repeat it, was a gift in disguise.

The Gift of Life

Trials also enable us to see that every moment we're alive is a gift from God. I was reminded of this a few years ago when our church staff went on a retreat to a lake house in the Catskills of New York. One afternoon our student ministries pastor, Matt, and I had the bright idea to paddle out to the middle of the lake in a canoe, in the forty-degree water, to fish. As we left the dock, another staff member laughed, "You're going to flip that thing."

We laughed and said, "No way."

Twenty minutes later we stopped paddling and let the canoe come to a rest in the middle of the lake. Then, as Matt turned around to face me, the canoe quickly moved to the right. I overcompensated by leaning to the left, and within seconds we were both underwater.

The first thing I heard was Matt coming up from under the water and gasping for air. We treaded water for a moment, assessed the situation, and knew we were in trouble. We tried to flip the canoe over but it was full of water. I said, "Matt, we've got to swim for it." So we grabbed our floatable seat cushions, which were of little help, and took off. As we swam, I wondered at one point if we'd make it—the water was freezing and choppy, the shore seemed too far away, and no other boats were near us to help. I remember praying, "Jesus, don't let us die in this lake." Finally, after praying and swimming for what seemed to be an eternity, we reached the shore. We struggled to stand up, hugged each other, and thanked God for sparing our lives.

Whenever I think back to that day in the water, I feel a twinge of anxiety in the pit of my stomach, but I've come to realize that this feeling is not necessarily a bad thing. That memory, along with dozens like it, serves a purpose in my life—to remind me that there are no guarantees. I don't walk this earth with a document signed by God in my back pocket, promising me a certain number of days on this earth. Each moment is a precious gift. Sometimes we forget this and race through life under the assumption that we or the ones we love will be sitting at the dinner table when we get home, which may not be the case.

The Bible says in James 4:14, "What is your life? You are a mist that appears for a little while and then vanishes." If this is the case, then we ought to be thankful for the trials God sends us. Hardship shakes us out of our routines. It makes us stop and reflect. Pain reminds us of our mortality, causing us to become more deliberate about the way we spend our time here on earth. As Thomas à Kempis said in his spiritual classic *The Imitation of Christ,* "It is good for us to encounter troubles and adversities from time to time, for trouble often compels a man to search his own heart. It reminds him that he is an exile here."[7]

Thornton Wilder's play *Our Town* reminds us how easily we lose perspective. The play is set in a small middle-American town at the beginning of the twentieth century. Its characters, Dr. and

Mrs. Gibbs, their son, George, and their daughter, Emily, live an uneventful, ordinary family life, until in act three, after many years have passed, Emily dies in childbirth along with her second child.

After she dies, Emily realizes that she and those she lived with breezed through life without any appreciation for its smaller moments, and she's consumed with remorse. Moved by her anguish, the "stage manager" in the play gives her an opportunity to go back and relive one day to the fullest. Emily picks her twelfth birthday. She quickly becomes disillusioned, however, by the way the people she interacts with callously rush through the entire day. Right before she must leave, she yells at her mother, "Oh, Mama, just look at me one minute as though you really saw me." Then she turns to the stage manager and says, "I can't. I can't go on. It goes so fast." Sobbing, she asks him through her tears, "Do any human beings ever realize life while they live it?—every, every minute?" He replies, "No. The saints and poets, maybe they do some."[8]

When I first read that play, I said to myself, *I'm not going to become like that mother.* So I pulled out my calendar and vigorously blocked out time to spend with God and the people close to me in my life. I did great, for about three weeks. Over time, the stresses of life and the monotony of one day after another dulled my resolve. I fell back into the same routine as before. I wasn't ignoring people; it was just that the intensity of experiencing life wasn't there. Then, coincidentally, every month or so it seemed, something bad happened—sometimes small, sometimes large—that helped me regain perspective again. After those events I looked into my daughters' eyes as though seeing them for the first time. I listened to my wife's words with greater anticipation. I prayed a little more fervently. I realized that this was not an accident. Even though my system for scheduling meaningful moments failed, God's didn't. Through every painful situation God handed me a special pair of glasses that allowed me to see that my life and the lives of those I love could end at any moment.

The Presence of God

A strange thing happens when we experience troubles and hardship—God can seem more alive and present to us *during* the difficulty than before it began. Sometimes, as I described in chapter one, God seems distant to us, and we wonder if we'll ever feel his presence again. But just as frequently the opposite occurs, and we feel God's presence *because* of the hardship, not in spite of it. The Bible assures us in Psalm 34:18, "The LORD is close to the brokenhearted."

This makes me think of my final year at Princeton Theological Seminary. In order to graduate, I had certain required courses. "Educational Psychology," not the most exciting course in the catalog, was one. The first day of class, Dr. James Loder, the professor, cheerfully introduced himself and shared his personal story of faith. Four minutes into his passionate story, he started to cry and I thought, *This guy's a Presbyterian—I didn't think Presbyterians cried!* I was instantly drawn to him.

Dr. Loder shared the story of how he, his wife, Arlene, and their two daughters were driving near Kingston, New York, when he pulled over to help an elderly woman fix a flat tire. Without warning, another car whose driver had fallen asleep at the wheel crashed into the car Dr. Loder was fixing and shoved it on top of his chest. In spite of his injuries, he never lost consciousness. He watched as his wife, barely five feet tall, placed her hands underneath the bumper and miraculously lifted the car off his chest, breaking a vertebra in the process. Dr. Loder later recalled in his book *The Transforming Moment:*

> As I roused myself from under the car, a steady surge of life was rushing through me, carrying with it two solid assurances. First, I knew how deeply I felt love for those around me, especially my family. My two daughters sat crying on the embankment, and a deep love reached out of me toward them. The second assurance was that this disaster had a purpose.[9]

With that conviction he was quickly rushed to the hospital where, as he was being wheeled into surgery, he invited the surgical staff to join him as he sang a few lines of the hymn "Fairest Lord Jesus." With medical treatment and lots of prayer, he fully recovered, losing only part of a thumb.

Dr. Loder described to our class how that incident marked him as a follower of Jesus. Rather than assuming God had left him, it became a moment that enabled him to sense God's presence in a way he had not experienced up to that point.

Perhaps you recall from your days in high school or college the teachings of psychologist Abraham Maslow and his "hierarchy of needs." Maslow was obsessed with discovering which situations in life enable someone to become fully alive as a human being. He called such situations "peak-experiences."[10] Essentially, what Maslow argued is that a person cannot reach a state of "self-actualization" until certain basic needs have been met. He illustrates this with a diagram in the shape of a triangle with food, water, and oxygen on the bottom and self-actualization at the top. Maslow argued that a person can't really think about personal fulfillment if she doesn't have food for the day. However, give that same person a good job and a roof over her head, and then she will have the personal energy and ability to think about things such as purpose in life. In order to experience a spiritual or emotional revelation of sorts, Maslow argued, you must address the basic struggles of life first.

The problem is that a three-thousand pound Oldsmobile falling on a man's chest doesn't fit real well into Maslow's neat triangle. Nor do tumors, bankruptcy, or other painful scenarios Christians tell me have drawn them closer to God. Jesus would say that Maslow has everything backwards. It's not when you are at the top of the triangle that you feel God's presence; it's when you are at the bottom.

Luke 6:20, 21 tells us Jesus looked at his followers and said, "Blessed are you who are poor, for yours is the kingdom of God. Blessed are you who hunger now, for you will be satisfied. Blessed are you who weep now, for you will laugh."

Blessed? When we are hungry and crying and broken? Jesus would say, "Absolutely." Blessed are you when you have a learning disability. Blessed are you when your spouse leaves you. Blessed are you when you are sued. Blessed are you when your life is falling apart. Why? Because the very things that bring us pain also become the portals through which we experience the presence of God.

In Genesis 32 we find a strange story that involves a man named Jacob wrestling a real live angel. Jacob was returning to his boyhood home to face his brother Esau, from whom he had been estranged for many years. An angel appeared and wrestled him to the ground. Surprisingly, Jacob held his own in the match as the two wrestled through the night. Somewhere toward morning, the angel "saw that he could not overpower him, [and] he touched the socket of Jacob's hip so that his hip was wrenched as he wrestled" (v. 25).

In other words, the angel, God's representative, wounded him. But Jacob didn't allow the wound to cause him to question God's goodness. Instead, his response allowed him to experience the "steady surge of life" Dr. Loder wrote about. We're told that this experience so profoundly changed Jacob that he coined a new name for the exact location of the fight: "Jacob called the place Peniel, saying, 'It is because I saw God face to face'" (v. 30).

I wonder if Jacob thought, *I never want people to forget this place. Not me, my children, or their children's children. What I learned here this day is too important to forget.* What did he learn? He learned that God's presence becomes a reality through our wounds. The name Peniel comes from the combination of two Hebrew words: *panim,* the Hebrew word for "face," and *El,* the Hebrew name for God.[11] *Panim* was used in two ways—to describe someone's literal face, or to describe someone's physical presence. That's why many times the Bible uses the phrase "face of God" to describe God's presence. His "face" becomes clear to us during painful moments.

The Importance of People

The final thing God allows us to see through suffering is the importance of people. Years ago I started a meaningful ceremony that I conduct at every rehearsal before each wedding I perform. I gather everyone in the wedding party—family and friends—in a circle and ask them to join hands. I talk about how special this event is for the couple in the circle and explain that having the approval and support of family and friends is more important than thousands of dollars of wedding presents.

Then I ask everyone in the circle to give the couple a priceless gift—to share a word of blessing from the heart. I turn to the person on my right and ask him to begin. By the fifth person in the circle, the entire group is bawling. I'm not talking about polite crying; I'm talking about snot-dripping-down-the-shirt bawling. Everyone's bawling—the cocky best man who isn't a Christian and wants to get drunk that night, divorced parents who haven't spoken in years, and especially the bride and groom themselves. It is a powerful experience.

At one wedding I performed years ago, the last person to speak was the bride's father. *What a perfect way to end this evening,* I thought. *He will give his daughter words she will remember the rest of her life.* Instead, he threw up his hands, laughed, and said, "Ditto." Then he flipped his head around and looked at me with a sheepish grin.

My heart broke for the bride. I couldn't believe it. I didn't know what to say. I awkwardly ended with prayer, but what I wanted to do was lean over and say, "Do you have any idea what this weekend means to your daughter? Do you have any idea what your approval means to her? All you can muster at this moment is 'Ditto'? Let's try this again."

I'm guessing the father soothed his conscience by reminding himself that he was sending his daughter and future son-in-law on an all-expense-paid honeymoon to Cancun. I knew the bride, however. I knew about the estrangement she felt toward her father because of his neglect over the years. I guarantee she would have traded the trip, the luxurious reception, and the tables stacked with expensive gifts, every last one of them, for just one word from his heart.

Contrast this with the time Jesus was asked what is the most important commandment. Without hesitation he answered, "'Love the Lord your God with all your heart and with all your soul and with all your mind.' This is the first and greatest commandment. And the second is like it: 'Love your neighbor as yourself'" (Matthew 22:37-39).

I think that if Jesus had been standing in that circle with that father, he wouldn't have hesitated, as I did, to say something. I think he would have stopped, shared that Scripture, and then graciously asked the man to speak again, this time from his heart.

Why? Jesus understood that the two most important things we do in life are to love God and love people. That's it. When we stray from these commands, he sometimes allows us to experience trials. Trials take his place and refocus our attention on what's important. They remind us how quickly we can lose people. They remind us that each person in our life is a gift.

When I think of people who really understand this, I always think of my friends who can't have children. Right now it takes both hands to count the number of couples I know who can't have children. I've talked with them, I've listened to their stories, I've prayed with them. For some reason God hasn't answered our prayers. I can't understand it. All of these couples are the kind of people you want to have kids, but for some reason it hasn't happened for them.

If I were to take these friends into the circle at that wedding rehearsal and ask the emotionally stunted father to step out of the way, what do you think my friends would say? I know what would happen: My friends would clear their throats, reach into their pockets, and gently put on a special pair of glasses—lenses and frames shaped by years of frustration, endless cycles of infertility treatments and miscarriages. These glasses firmly in place, they would look the bride squarely in the eyes, smile, and then share an unending stream of blessings that would have made that young woman's heart dance.

Trials have a way of doing that. Trials have a way of allowing us to see what's really important in life.

NOTES

[1]Abraham Heschl, *Who Is Man?* (Stanford: Stanford University Press, 1965), 14.

[2]Madeleine L'Engle, *Walking on Water: Reflections on Faith and Art* (Colorado Springs: Waterbrook Press, 2004), 62.

[3]Leo Tolstoy, translated by Aylmer Maude and J. D. Duff, *The Death of Ivan Ilyich and Other Stories* (New York: Penguin Putnam, 2003), 148.

[4]Gerhard Kittel and Gerhard Friedrich, eds., translated by Geoffrey W. Bromiley, *Theological Dictionary of the New Testament, Abridged* (Grand Rapids: Eerdmans, 1985), 459.

[5]Simone Weil, translated by Arthur Wills, *Gravity and Grace* (New York: G. P. Putnam's Sons, 1952), 131.

[6]Jonathan Swift, *Gulliver's Travels* (New York: Penguin Putnam, 1999), 25.

[7]Thomas á Kempis, translated by Leo Sherley-Price, *The Imitation of Christ* (New York: Penguin Books, 1952), 39.

[8]Thornton Wilder, *Our Town* (New York: HarperCollins, 1965), 108.

[9]James Loder, *The Transforming Moment* (Colorado Springs: Helmers & Howard, 1989), 10.

[10]See A. H. Maslow, *Religions, Value, and Peak-Experiences* (New York: Penguin Group, 1994).

[11]R. Laird Harris, Gleason L. Archer, Jr., and Bruce K. Waltke, eds., *Theological Wordbook of the Old Testament* (Chicago: Moody Press, 1980), vol. 2, 727.

7

Witness

The greatest converting influence of all is a life which clearly and obviously is possessed of a power which can cope with the human situation in all its problems, in all its tragedy, and in all its pain.

—William Barclay

This and the final chapter of this book may be the two most important, because both deal with matters of eternity. C. S. Lewis said, "A book on suffering which says nothing of heaven, is leaving out almost the whole of one side of the account. Scripture and tradition habitually put the joys of heaven into the scale against the sufferings of earth, and no solution of the problem of pain which does not do so can be called a Christian one."[2]

I agree with Lewis, and in chapter eleven I will attempt to describe what Heaven will be like, but I feel compelled to add one thing to Lewis's observation: a book on suffering that says nothing about *Hell* leaves out a good part of the account as well. Jesus, his first followers, and the tradition of the early church made it quite clear that Hell is a reality to be avoided at all costs. They also made it clear that our experience of pain and suffering can be used by God to help those who are not yet Christians to avoid it.

One of the reasons I lost my faith in graduate school, which I wrote about in chapter one, was over this very issue. I just couldn't bring myself to fully embrace what the Bible teaches about Hell. My first problem had to do with the character of God. How could a loving God send people to a place of eternal torment? It seemed logically inconsistent to me. If God is love, wouldn't he want to spend eternity with all those he created, not just a few?

Second, I had a hard time with the issue of fairness. How could my friends of other faiths hear the message of Jesus, choose not to accept it, live a devout life maybe even more moral than my own, and still be sent to Hell after they die? Didn't I become a Christian in part because I grew up in a Christian family, and didn't they become Buddhist, Bahá'í, or Islamic in part because of the early influences of their families as well? Hell seemed like a penalty for being born in the wrong place at the wrong time.

Another problem I had with Hell was it seemed that the punishment was disproportionate to the crime. How could Jesus send someone to a place of everlasting pain and torture for refusing to become his follower during this brief lifetime? It seemed tantamount to sending a person to death row for stealing a postage stamp.

My final problem with Hell was very pragmatic: I believed that the ultraconservative fundamentalists of the Christian community had a corner market on preaching Hell, and I would rather have died than be associated with them in any way at the time.

When I returned to Christianity after almost one year of wandering and searching, I returned with all of my heart but was still unconvinced of the existence of Hell. Because I was graduating and hoped to become a pastor, this created a serious dilemma, so I came up with what seemed like a simple solution: I would never tell anyone about my predicament. In fact, I carried my secret around for four years after graduate school without ever telling anyone, not my church and staff in Ohio, not my friends, not even my wife. The secret was so well hidden that sometimes I was able to forget about it. One day, however, God decided it was time to bring the matter out in the open and confront it head on.

AN UNEXPECTED CONFRONTATION

I was in the habit of going to a monastery roughly once a month for a spiritual retreat. I would arrive early in the day to pray, journal, and take long walks in the woods, and leave late in the afternoon. (Ironically enough for a Protestant, I've found that some of my greatest spiritual insights have come while visiting Catholic monasteries.) On one such retreat I felt an overwhelming sense of spiritual pressure, the spiritual equivalent of the kind of pressure you feel in your ears when you are swimming in deep water. I could sense something was wrong but didn't know what it was. For the better part of the day, I locked myself into a cold, cement-block room and asked God to show me the source of my consternation.

For the first three hours, I heard nothing—my prayers seemed like they were bouncing off the ceiling. By around noon I felt like I was really starting to make a connection with God, but I wasn't prepared for what happened next, when I felt God's Spirit impress upon my heart, "Brian, you're a pastor and your job is to teach people the Bible, but you don't believe what you're teaching. You don't believe in Hell."

I was a little startled so I picked up my Bible and played what I call "Bible Roulette." I closed my eyes, fanned the pages, and randomly pointed to passages and read them. The first passage was about eternal punishment. I looked up at the ceiling and said, "That's a coincidence." The second passage was about God's wrath. This time I felt a little uneasy. Then I did it a third time and my finger landed on a passage about judgment day. I'm not usually the most mystical person in the world, but I slowly closed the pages of my Bible, sat it down on the table next to me and said, "I get the message." Church leaders must "keep hold of the deep truths of the faith with a clear conscience" (1 Timothy 3:9), and Hell is one of those "deep truths."

I spent the next five hours reading and underlining every passage about Hell in the New Testament, and as I did I felt an overwhelming sense of conviction. What I discovered shocked me. I had always assumed that the Bible contained only a few scattered references to Hell. I was wrong; it is taught everywhere. Take the book of Matthew, for instance, just one book among twenty-seven in the entire New Testament. Here is what we learn about Hell from that book alone:

Thirteen separate passages record Jesus' teachings about the judgment of nonbelievers and their assignment to eternal punishment.[3] Matthew 13:49, 50 summarizes them all: "This is how it will be at the end of the age. The angels will come and separate the wicked from the righteous and throw them into the fiery furnace, where there will be weeping and gnashing of teeth."

Jesus employed the most graphic language to describe what Hell is like: *fire* (vv. 5:22; v. 18:9); *eternal fire* (v. 18:8); *destruction* (v. 7:13); *away from his presence* (v. 7:23); *thrown outside* (vv. 8:12; 22:13; 25:30); *fiery furnace* (v. 13:42); *darkness* (vv. 22:13; 25:30); *eternal punishment* (v. 25:46); *weeping and gnashing of teeth* (vv. 8:12; 13:42; 13:50; 22:13; 24:51).

Jesus twice used *eternal* (vv. 18:8; 25:46) to convey that the punishment of nonbelievers would continue forever.

As I moved from the Gospels into the rest of the New Testament, I was struck by how the writers unashamedly addressed the issue. There was no hesitancy or apology in their words. The basic tone was, "This is a reality. Now let's get out there and tell people how to avoid it." Second Thessalonians 1:7-9 summarizes what these other New Testament authors taught:

> This will happen when the Lord Jesus is revealed from heaven in blazing fire with his powerful angels. He will punish those who do not know God and do not obey the gospel of our Lord Jesus. They will be punished with everlasting destruction and shut out from the presence of the Lord and from the majesty of his power.

My heart raced as I flipped page after page after page. I discovered, by the end of my study, that the New Testament's teaching about Hell is not an ambiguous topic supported by a few hard-to-understand passages. It is inescapable: virtually every book in the New Testament underscores some aspect of the reality of Hell. Jesus taught it, early church leaders taught it, but I wasn't teaching it. I realized I had a decision to make. Could I discount what Jesus taught about Hell if I based my belief in Heaven on similar passages in the same books?

Could it be possible that Jesus' disciples actually had the same reservations I had, but still persisted in teaching it because they knew in the depths of their soul that Hell was real? Could it be that my hesitancy to believe in Hell was really a sign of my compassion for people? Yet, if Hell really exists, and I knew that but wasn't willing to tell people how to avoid it, wouldn't that also be the most extreme form of cruelty imaginable? Most of all, could it be that I was ultimately basing my acceptance of this teaching more on what people would think of me than whether I felt it was intellectually plausible?

A NEW BEGINNING

I closed my Bible, dropped to my knees on the monastery floor, and cried out to God. I asked Jesus for forgiveness for my lack of commitment to the truth contained in the Bible. I rushed home and called together my leadership team and church staff and told them about my experience. I apologized for failing them as their pastor and asked for their forgiveness. That Sunday I stood before my congregation and asked for their forgiveness as well. I pledged my commitment to teach the Bible, every last bit of it. It was a humbling turning point in my calling as a Christian and a pastor.

Afterward I experienced a sudden and intense passion to introduce people to Jesus. No longer did I want to talk to people about spiritual matters to get them to join our church or help them reach higher levels of spiritual awareness; I wanted to change the eternal trajectory of their lives. The intensity of my prayer life changed dramatically. Conversations at gas stations and restaurants took on a whole new meaning. I began to feel God's presence as I initiated spiritual conversations and built relationships with people far from God. For the first time ever, I began to see people through an eternal lens. No longer was a parent on my kids' soccer team simply "Jack Smith, husband, father of three, regional manager, and avid golfer." He became Jack Smith, a person deeply loved by God, headed for eternal darkness, and sent into my life by God to introduce him and his family to Jesus.

The most profound thing that happened to me as a result of this experience was my change in attitude toward pain and suffering. I had read in the Bible that God uses our pain as a catalyst to cause others to become interested in spiritual matters, but I never really took those passages seriously. After my experience in the monastery, it became clear why: if there were no Hell, then there was no reason for believers to endure pain and suffering to help others become Christians. Without the existence of Hell, don't we all end up in the same place anyway? Why joyfully endure pain if it has no larger purpose beyond what we experience here on earth?

After coming to a biblically sound position, however, I began to view personal struggles in a new light. Because I now believed Hell existed and that those who do not become followers of Jesus go there, I was willing to use any means necessary, even enduring pain and suffering, to motivate others to seek Jesus. I began to view my pain and struggles as one more way Jesus could draw people to himself.

HOW GOD USES OUR PAIN

Transformed into Fellow Strugglers

Our pain can draw people to Jesus when it changes us so we can deliver the message about the afterlife in a way God himself would want it to be communicated. When we first become Christians, we're not exactly the most ideal candidates to handle public relations for the Almighty. If the president of the United States searches far and wide for the best and brightest people to serve as his go-between with the public, you would think that the creator of the universe would copy his idea, but God seems quite content using people like you and me.

I often wonder why Jesus didn't commission angels to be his spokespeople. In the Old Testament, when God wanted to communicate a message that he didn't want to get messed up, he always sent an angel. In fact, the Greek word in the New Testament that is translated "angel" is *angelos,* which actually means "messenger."[4] When God needed to get an important message to Abraham and Sarah about the birth of their son, what did he do? He sent angels. When he wanted to communicate battle plans to Gideon? Same thing. When he announced the birth of Jesus, who did he send? You got it, angels. So why the change of plans? After his crucifixion and resurrection, Jesus told his disciples, "As the Father has sent me, I am sending you" (John 20:21), and every eyebrow in the room had to be raised. "What? You're sending us? No angels?" What was Jesus thinking? Why send Joe Smith from Atlanta or Brian Jones from Philly or Jane Doe from Indianapolis when you have angels like Michael and Gabriel on standby? Angels never get scared and rarely forget their lines. There is also the added benefit that angels can't be beaten up or killed.

My guess is that Jesus knew that the decision to become a Christian would be more genuine if a human being learned how to do so from another human being. Perhaps Jesus didn't want people to feel coerced into signing up to follow him and knew that sending an intimidating creature the size of a middle linebacker wouldn't really accomplish that. Yet he also had to know the potential for communication problems. He knew that we humans tend to be arrogant and petty and that we could dilute the message or change it altogether.

For example, when we lived in Ohio, we had the opportunity to visit another church in our community. During the service the pastor announced that it was time for the children in the church to come forward for a children's sermon. As our daughters went forward and sat near the podium with the other children, I smiled and thought, *This should be nice. We don't do this at our church.* I noticed that behind the pastor was a hammer dangling by its two claws on the edge of a table. Attached to the handle of the hammer was a piece of string that dropped down to the floor and then ran up the pastor's leg and into his pocket. A Barbie doll was directly under the hammer.

The pastor started his sermon by asking, "Boys and girls, can anyone tell me what the word *sin* means?"

One girl raised her hand and said, "I have a new hamster!"

The pastor smiled and said, "That's nice, Samantha" and offered his own definition. Then he asked if anyone knew what the word *Hell* meant.

I whispered, to no one in particular, "These are preschoolers. Where is he going with this?"

No one could provide an answer to the pastor's second question either, so he provided his own. Five minutes into this "children's sermon," the pastor said in a loud, commanding voice, "Boys and girls, this is what happens when we sin against God and refuse to become Christians!" and he pulled the string attached to the hammer. The children lunged backwards and screamed as the hammer crashed down on top of the doll below. My wife, whose view was blocked, leaned over and asked, "What happened?"

I said, "God just killed Barbie." I thought about standing up and interrupting the guy, but my wife talked me out of it. After his message I grabbed my kids and we walked out the door, praying that there weren't any non-Christians in the room that day.

This is one reason why God allows us to go through pain and suffering—to keep us from becoming like that pastor. God wants us to communicate clearly what happens after we die, but not as if we enjoy it. Years ago a wise Christian told me that I should never talk about Hell without pain in my voice and tears in my eyes. This is advice worth remembering. It's too easy to become flippant and arrogant when we talk about this awful place, as if there were no difference between a discussion about Hell and a football game on television. When we talk about Hell, we are talking about *real* people going there: neighbors, friends, family members, loved ones. We should be heartbroken. We should lose sleep over this. It should consume us with uneasiness the way it consumed Jesus and his first followers.

Pain helps us interact with people who are far from God the way God himself interacts with them. In John 16:7, 8, Jesus said:

But very truly I tell you, it is for your good that I am going
away. Unless I go away, the Advocate will not come to you; but
if I go, I will send him to you. When he comes, he will prove
the world to be in the wrong about sin and righteousness and
judgment (TNIV).

The Advocate is the Holy Spirit, the third person of the Trinity.
God's Spirit is pictured here as someone who would come to earth
to "take over" for Jesus after he left. Unlike Jesus, who as a human
was physically bound to one location at a time, the Advocate,
without a physical body, could be present all over the world at
once. This is why Jesus indicates that it was actually better for
him to leave his disciples—more people could directly encounter
God's presence after his departure than if he stayed. The Advocate's
job, "to prove the world to be in the wrong," might strike us as
rather harsh, a lot like the hellfire-and-brimstone children's homily
preacher, but nothing could be further from the truth.

The word translated "Advocate" is the Greek word *parakletos,*
which is a combination of two Greek words: *para,* meaning
"beside," and *kalein,* meaning "to call."[5] A *parakletos* is someone
who is "called" to "come to the side of" someone. Other versions
of the Bible accurately translate this word "Comforter." The image
that immediately comes to mind is a row of people sitting arm in
arm alongside a widow offering as much comfort and support as
they can possibly muster.

Pain helps us assume this posture with people who are not yet
Christians by letting us experience what spiritual writer Thomas
Merton called "an evisceration, a gutting and scouring of the
human soul."[6] Pain humbles us and breaks us so thoroughly that
we become almost incapable of delivering a spiritual message in a

condescending manner. Pain acts like a spiritual abrasive: it scours us. It lowers our gaze, slows our steps, and bends our spiritual back. Pain can turn the proudest of Christians into a *parakletos*. This is what happened to me.

I've grown to the point where I really resonate with the last written words of Martin Luther, the man who instigated the beginning of the Protestant Reformation in the sixteenth century. Luther, by all accounts, is arguably one of the most influential Christian leaders and thinkers the church has ever produced, yet Luther's life was one long journey of affliction. Persecuted by the Catholic Church, tormented by personal demons, carrying the pressure of leading a newly emerging church movement—by the end of his life he was a broken man. Among the endless volumes of books, sermons, and letters this brilliant man left to the church, Luther penned these poignant final words: "We are beggars: this is true."[7]

A few years ago our church in Philadelphia went through our first crisis: French-kissing homosexuals in the worship service. One day after services a man in our church's band approached me and said, "Dude, I just saw my first homosexual kiss!" I said, "Where?" He pointed to the auditorium and said they had been French kissing during the worship service. I said, "Really? I didn't see them." I looked for other staff members, but they said they hadn't witnessed it either. The next Sunday three people came up to me and said they had seen the same thing. This went on for weeks. It was like the homosexual version of "Where's Waldo?" During the sermon I would slowly scan the audience looking for lip-locking visitors, but to no avail.

Eventually, for reasons I could never discover, our frisky friends left, but not before I received a nasty e-mail from a woman visiting from another church that saw the couple making out. She asked, "Is your church the kind of church that welcomes homosexuals?" That was a loaded question. I e-mailed back and outlined our church's belief that homosexuality, like all other sins, goes against what is clearly taught in the Bible. I also explained that we would welcome anyone, regardless of their background, to be a part of our church service, jokingly adding that we had a very strict policy against all French kissing during the service—homosexual or heterosexual. I concluded my e-mail by saying, "I have to be honest; I was glad to hear that two homosexuals felt comfortable enough to attend our church services and weren't scared away by the adulterers, pornographers, tax cheats, liars and other messed-up people in the seats around them."

I knew this was a defining moment in the life of our church. It would either swing our church culture toward legalism or toward grace. Wanting to use this situation as a teaching moment, the following Sunday I read the woman's e-mail and my response in the middle of my sermon. When I finished, the entire room erupted with applause. We now have a large, professionally designed sign placed at the front door of our church services so every visitor that joins us will see it: "No perfect people allowed."

Courage in the Face of Death

Another way God uses our pain to draw people to Jesus is by allowing them to see our courage in the face of death. I was reminded of this one evening as I was reading a collection of ancient Christian documents from the second century. In a letter historians call "The Epistle to Diognetus," an unknown second-century follower of Jesus wrote to a non-Christian skeptic named

Diognetus to answer his questions about this strange new religion called Christianity. The opening lines of his letter capture what Diognetus must have found so appealing about followers of Jesus roughly eighteen hundred years ago:

> I have noticed, my lord Diognetus, the deep interest you have been showing in Christianity, and the close and careful inquiries you have been making about it. You would like to know what God Christians believe in, and what sort of cult they practice which enables them to set so little store by this world, and even to make light of death itself . . . I pray God, the Author of both our speech and hearing, to grant me such use of my tongue that you may derive the fullest benefit from listening to me.[8]

As I read those opening lines, I was struck by the phrase "make light of death," and I wondered what Diognetus had seen that made him form this impression of Christians. Maybe Diognetus had a Christian neighbor who risked her life every day as she walked through dangerous streets feeding the poor. Maybe he watched a close friend with a terminal disease live his final days full of joy, praying to a God whose name Diognetus didn't recognize. Maybe he watched a mob of people in the marketplace attack a Christian family because they were hurting business by refusing to purchase meat that had been sacrificed to one of the pagan gods. We're not told what specific event caused Diognetus to become so curious about Christianity. All we know is that he was curious to know why these people could smile in the face of death.

In my experience, courage in the face of death is what ultimately separates Christians from non-Christians. One of the best sermon series I have ever preached was a series called "Dangerous Prayers." I kicked off the series with a sermon on Psalm 39:4, which says, "Show me, O LORD, my life's end and the number of my days; let me know how fleeting is my life." The series was aimed at people who were not yet Christians, so I spent a long time trying to figure out how I could get them to reflect upon "how fleeting" their life is.

After a few days I came up with what I thought was a pretty creative idea. We called a local funeral home and borrowed one of their caskets. Right before the sermon that Sunday, the lights went dark. The ushers brought lit candelabras onto the stage, and funeral music began playing in the background. In the hallway I jumped into the casket and the ushers closed the coffin lid and slowly carried the casket onto the stage. I timed it so the coffin sat on the stage for two full minutes before I slowly lifted the creaking lid and crawled out with my Bible and sermon notes.

For almost thirty minutes I spoke with the lights off and the candles glowing. I told my listeners that I could predict with one hundred percent accuracy that each of them was going to end up in a coffin one day. It might be twenty, thirty, or forty years before it happens, but they could count on it coming.

Our people have come to expect the unexpected at our church, so I thought I would receive an endless number of high fives and "Great sermon, Pastor" comments in the hallway. Quite the contrary! People were fuming. Rather, the non-Christians who attended our church, roughly half of our attendance at the time, were fuming. They came unglued, which was a good thing. I had more spiritual conversations that week with people who wanted to know how they could face death with courage and peace than after any other sermon I've ever preached.

Recently I reflected on the names of the people that I have personally had the privilege of helping become followers of Jesus. As I came across each of their names, I was incredibly moved because each one reminds me of a beautiful story of grace and redemption. I'll never forget:

• The businessman who yelled, "Sign me the %$#@ up! I'm going for it!" during my backswing on the eleventh hole of the local golf course;

• Seven-year-old Alyssa, whose tender voice and infectious smile reminded me of everything that was right in the world;

• The hippie from a rock band who became a Christian and then told me he couldn't wait to have sex with a Christian girl. When I told him the Bible says he'd have to wait until he was married, he said, "You're kidding, right?";

• The star high school wrestler whose father's absence left a hole in his soul so large you could drive a truck through it;

• The man with autism whose former church refused to baptize him because he couldn't recite the confessional formula exactly they way they had written it.

From time to time I'll stop to think about what people far from God are looking for: Answers? An experience? Healing? Friends? Acceptance? I can't speak for everyone, only the people I've helped become Christians, but in my experience, people far from God are looking for one thing: the ability to look death in the eye and smile. They want hope. They want to know that there's more to this world than a life that vanishes quicker than smoke from a fire.

This explains, better than anything else, why God allows us to go through rough stretches in our lives. He knows that Heaven and Hell hang in the balance. He sees people tumbling towards

a Christless eternity and is furiously trying to capture their
attention. Sometimes, in a last-ditch effort to draw their gaze
away from the world, God will allow *us* to walk into a dark place
so our non-Christian family and friends can see how we respond
to it. There's a reason for the trials and pain we go through, and it
isn't a funny-sounding theological phrase, but rather the names of
people we know: Larry in accounting; Jeff in your bowling league;
Wendy who works down the hall; your husband, John; your wife,
Annette. They're watching us. More accurately, they're hungering
for something we have, and sometimes the only way they'll get
a glimpse of it is when they see us stumble into situations where
we can "make light of death." Historians have often marveled at
how the church has grown the fastest when it has been persecuted
the most. This may be because people who are far from God
intuitively sense that the only person who can show them how to
truly live is the person who is not afraid to die.

NOTES

[1] William Barclay, *Turning to God* (London: The Epworth Press, 1963), 41.

[2] C. S. Lewis, *The Problem of Pain* (New York: HarperCollins, 1996), 148.

[3] See Matthew 7:21-23; 8:12; 10:15, 33; 11:22-24; 12:41, 42; 13:30, 40-43, 49, 50; 24:50, 51; 25:11, 12, 29, 30, 31-46.

[4] Gerhard Kittel and Gerhard Friedrich, eds., translated by Geoffrey W. Bromiley, *Theological Dictionary of the New Testament, Abridged* (Grand Rapids: Eerdmans, 1985), 12.

[5] Ibid., 782.

[6] Thomas Merton, edited by Thomas P. McDonnell, *A Thomas Merton Reader* (New York: Doubleday, 1989), 313.

[7] Dr. Martin Luthers Werke, *The Last Written Words of Luther: Holy Ponderings of the Reverend Father Doctor Martin Luther,* translated by James A. Kellerman (Weimar: Hermann Boehlaus Nachfolger, 1909), http://www.iclnet. org/pub/resources/text/wittenburg/luther/beggars.txt

[8] "The Epistle to Diognetus" in *Early Christian Writings* (New York, NY: Viking Penguin, Inc., 1987), 142.

8

Mystery

Hope is a woman whose presence fills
whatever room the demons leave.

—Liesel M. Tarquini

Whenever my cousin Craig and I got together, our parents
knew trouble wasn't far behind. Craig was two years younger
than me and lived in Grayson, Kentucky, not too far from where
my family lived in Columbus, Ohio. Once a month Craig's dad
traveled to Ohio on business. Fortunately for me the whole family
came with him and spent the weekend with my grandparents,
who lived near us.

I always begged my parents to let me spend the night at
my grandparents' house on those weekends. I have two sisters,
no brothers, and Craig became like a younger brother to me.
Together we fished, dug up worms, walked to the corner Dairy

Mart to get ice cream, terrorized the neighbor's dog, played pinball, threw rocks at birds, and played basketball.

We loved playing basketball. One weekend we pulled my grandparents' ladder out of their garage, stood on the top of it, and slammed basketballs into the basket so hard that the rim eventually broke. Despite our occasional destructiveness, my grandfather never complained. I think he enjoyed having rambunctious boys around the house. My grandmother, on the other hand, probably still goes to therapy a few times a week!

Needless to say, I was pretty excited when I began my freshman year at Kentucky Christian University, located in the town where Craig lived. Almost immediately we began hunting and doing other things together, just like when we were kids. One weekend, however, as I drove home to spend time with my parents, I was completely unaware of the tragedy that was unfolding back in Kentucky.

On Saturday morning, as we were sitting around the house after breakfast, my mom answered the phone. Seconds later she dropped whatever she was holding and started to shake convulsively. She buried the phone in her chest and cried out, "Craig is dead! He drowned at Carter Lake."

I was dazed. I stood up and paced back and forth in the kitchen, listening to my mother talk to my aunt. I couldn't believe it. When I couldn't stand what I was hearing any longer, I ran to my room and sobbed.

We later learned that Craig had been fishing in a boat with two friends, one who could swim and one who could not. After they paddled to the middle of the lake, the boat started to take on water. Craig told his friend who could swim to help their other friend to shore and said he would grab the equipment and meet them on the bank. In the scurry to gather their rods and tackle, the hooks and fishing line from their poles wrapped around his legs and got caught on the inside of the boat. Craig was unable to free himself when the boat submerged. His two friends ran to the nearest house and called the police, and my uncle, who was the local fire chief, was one of the people who responded to the call, not knowing it was his own son he was being sent to rescue. When he arrived at the lake, paramedics were in the process of giving CPR to Craig, but it was too late.

The following week at the viewing at the funeral home, long lines of people wrapped around the building, waiting to get inside. High school students were everywhere, in small groups every few feet, holding each other and crying. Flowers were piled in every available space. When I reached my aunt and uncle, who were seated on a couch to the right of the casket, I began to cry so hard I couldn't stand up. My uncle sat me down on the edge of the couch, next to my aunt, while he and Craig's younger brother, Todd, got up and stood next to the casket. I held my aunt's hand and kept repeating, "I can't believe this is happening. This can't be happening."

The funeral the next day was held in the gymnasium of Craig's high school because so many people wanted to attend. Area fire trucks were parked outside to lead the procession to the burial site. When we arrived at the cemetery, the uphill walk to the burial site was slow. The pastor ended his graveside talk with "ashes to ashes; dust to dust," and then he prayed a comforting prayer. As people paraded by my aunt and uncle, giving their final condolences, I noticed a hawk flying above the trees in the distance. Cars were driving past the cemetery on I-64, just a few miles from my college campus. To everyone except the people standing on that hillside, it was just another beautiful, sunny day.

Late the following evening I went outside for a walk and noticed a portable basketball hoop had been set up in the campus parking lot. With an adjustable rim set at nine feet instead of the standard ten, it was low enough for me to dunk on it. Rain began as I was shooting, but I kept going. For the next hour I dunked basketballs, just like Craig and I used to do when we were kids. I hit the rim of the basket so hard my hands and wrists started to bleed. The more basketballs I dunked, the angrier I became. The harder it poured, the harder I hit the rim. Suddenly, as if someone turned off a valve in the sky, the rain stopped. I grabbed the ball, wiped the blood on my pants, looked up at the stars and said to God, "I hate you," and walked back to my dorm room.

GOD'S SILENCE

Jean-Paul Sartre is the only writer I know who has verbalized what I felt that night. In Sartre's play *The Devil and the Good Lord*, a former soldier named Goetz converts to Christianity but over time becomes disillusioned with his faith. In one scene, Goetz says:

> I supplicated, I demanded a sign, I sent messages to Heaven, no reply. Heaven ignored my very name. Each minute I wondered what I could BE in the eyes of God. Now I know the answer: nothing. God does not see me, God does not hear me, God does not know me. You see this emptiness over our heads? That is God. You see this gap in the door? It is God. You see that hole in the ground? That is God again. Silence is God. Absence is God. God is the loneliness of man.[2]

If that's what I felt that night, I can only imagine what my aunt and uncle were feeling.

So far in this book, we've looked at how God uses trials and hardships in our lives to accomplish five different areas of spiritual transformation. Through our trials:

We develop greater levels of compassion for those around us;

We experience God's power in ways we normally wouldn't;

We are enabled to see people, circumstances, God, and the world differently;

We develop deeper levels of faith.

People far from God witness our perseverance and joy and are prompted to inquire about the source of our strength.

God's concern with each of these areas of spiritual transformation makes some sense, as long as you're not the one pulling your son from the bottom of a lake, taking your wife off life support, or walking out of a rape crisis center. There are times, however, when our hardships defy any attempts at categorization. There are times when the pain we live through is so intense, the circumstances so heinous, the situation so meaningless that any effort to justify it, explain it, or bring God into the conversation brings us to the point of utter rage. As C. S. Lewis once said, "Sometimes it is hard not to say 'God forgive God.'"[3]

EMBRACING MYSTERY

In the New Testament there is a word that is used to describe the painful experience of God's silence. It's the word *mystery.* We typically think of a mystery as a type of book or movie, but the Bible uses the term to describe aspects of a human being's experience with God. *Mystery* comes from the Greek word *myo*, which means "to shut the mouth."[4] The New Testament uses it to describe how God kept the person and work of Jesus a secret for thousands of years, hidden from people up until the moment he appeared in the first century.[5] Specific teachings that were kept hidden from God's people, only to be revealed and explained by the apostles, are also described as a mystery.[6] In a similar way, mystery can be a larger metaphor for what we experience when God chooses to "keep his mouth shut" when he has allowed horrible things to happen to us.

One of the most painful but beautiful things to witness in life is a person grappling with mystery. Over the years I've met people who have lived through indescribable circumstances, called out to God for answers but were met by silence, yet still chose to continue to follow him. Take, for example, a family in a church I served who had a burglar break into their home in the middle of the night while everyone was sleeping, put a pillow over their oldest son's mouth, and violate him. The perpetrator was never caught. Week after week that family went to therapy and week after week, somehow, they kept coming to church. I was astounded by how they were able to keep going. The mother told me, "Brian, I'm not even going to ask why this happened to my son. There is no answer. I'm not giving up, though. God's all we've got right now."

Perhaps God has sent you to live in this harsh place called mystery. If so, I want to introduce you to the book of Psalms. In the Bible, the book of Psalms is a collection of prayers written down and gathered by God's people over twenty-five hundred years ago. What's interesting about the psalms is the wide range of human emotions they express. In Psalm 25:1 we find someone tenderly praying, "To you, O LORD, I lift up my soul," but in Psalm 74:1 we find someone else screaming, "Why have you rejected us forever, O God?" I believe one of the reasons the psalms were included in the Bible was to teach us how to take our pain into the presence of God. That's probably why in the fourth century, St. Ambrose called the psalms the "gymnasium" of the soul.[7] The psalms have always been the place where hurting Christians have gone to work through their feelings of rage and frustration.

PSALMS OF LAMENT

One thing I encourage you to do if you're living in mystery is to read the book of Psalms from beginning to end. Since there are one hundred fifty psalms in all, you can read five psalms each morning or evening and finish the whole collection in one month's time. When you do this, take special notice of the "psalms of lament." Biblical scholars use that term for those psalms prayed by those living in mystery. Our English word *lament* comes from the Latin word for weeping.[8] Psalms 6, 13, 22, 35, 42, 43, 88, 102, 109, and 137 are examples of this type of psalm. You'll know you've come across one when you feel like you've turned the corner in a hallway and bumped into someone kicking, punching, and screaming at a locked door; the psalms of lament are that intense.

When you find a psalm of lament that expresses what you're feeling, take that psalm and read it out loud to God. Pray that psalm. Read it with as much force and anger and depth as you can muster. A mentor of mine once told me that when I'm unable to pray, I should let someone else pray for me—let the psalms become your prayers.

The reason I think it is so important to pray the psalms while we are living in mystery is to learn how to be honest with God. Looking back, I'm amazed at how honest I was with God *before* I became a Christian. Before my conversion I held nothing back; whatever I felt at the time, I expressed it to God. After becoming a Christian, however, it was as if someone slipped me a little note that told me to use my manners when I approach the Almighty. For quite some time, when I was troubled or angry with God, I never told him about it—I didn't think I was allowed. This resulted in an inconsistency between what was in my heart and what came out of my mouth. The psalms of lament gave me the courage to be real.

If the psalms of lament teach us anything, it is this: Christians can love God and feel immense hatred toward him at the same time. God doesn't want tamed down, sanitized, forcibly dishonest prayers. He wants us to talk to him from our hearts, and sometimes that involves screaming and using words we wouldn't repeat in public. Sometimes anything less than this is dishonest.

Three Parts of a Lament

As you read through the psalms of lament, you will notice that the people who wrote these prayers tended to focus on three basic themes: accusations against God, hatred toward enemies, and vows of praise. Ironically, these three themes are noticeably absent in modern-day books, sermons, and seminars on prayer. This might explain why there is such a hunger for direction on how to hold on to God when life becomes unbearable. Much of what passes as prayer these days is nothing more than positive thinking and self-talk, rather than authentic communication with the living God. Let's take a look at what dominated the prayers of ancient saints living in mystery.

Accusations against God. The first thing we notice when we read the psalms of lament is that those praying felt free to accuse God of not caring about them. Their accusations are, at times, brutal. In Psalm 44:24, God is asked, "Why do you hide your face and forget our misery and oppression?" When I first read that, as a new Christian, I couldn't believe someone could be that brash with God and live to write it. Yet, Psalm 44:23 is even worse: "Awake, O Lord! Why do you sleep? Rouse yourself! Do not reject us forever." The author essentially tells God to wipe the sleep from his eyes and quit being lazy! How could these psalm writers talk this way?

I think the reason they were so bold is because they were willing to be honest. They wrote what they felt. If the psalms are the gymnasium of the soul, then I think the psalms of lament are the personal trainers—pushing us to shed our inhibitions and false humility and encouraging us to express what we genuinely feel in our hearts toward God.

In his book *Night*, concentration camp survivor Elie Wiesel tells about the time three of his fellow prisoners, two men and a small young boy, were accused of blowing up a Nazi power station:

> The SS seemed more preoccupied, more disturbed than usual. To hang a young boy in front of thousands of spectators was no light matter. The head of the camp read the verdict. All eyes were on the child. He was lividly pale, almost calm, biting

his lips. The gallows threw its shadow over him.

This time the Lagerkapo [the usual guard] refused to act as executioner. Three SS replaced him.

The three victims mounted together onto the chairs. The three necks were placed at the same moment within the nooses. "Long live liberty!" cried the two adults.

But the child was silent.

"Where is God? Where is He?" someone behind me asked.

At a sign from the head of the camp, the three chairs tipped over.

Total silence throughout the camp. On the horizon, the sun was setting. "Bare your heads!" yelled the head of the camp. His voice was raucous. We were weeping.

"Cover your heads!" Then the march past began. The two adults were no longer alive. Their tongues hung swollen, blue-tinged. But the third rope was still moving; being so light, the child was still alive.

For more than half an hour he stayed there, struggling between life and death, dying in slow agony under our eyes. And we had to look him full in the face. He was still alive when I passed in front of him. His tongue was still red, his eyes were not yet glazed.

Behind me, I heard the same man asking: "Where is God now?" And I heard a voice within me answer him: "Where is He? Here He is—He is hanging here on this gallows."[9]

You know what I appreciate about Wiesel's excruciating words? They were real. He didn't care about how they would sound or if they were theologically correct. This is what he felt. How about you? What has caused you pain? What has made you want to end your life? What has so completely broken your soul that you wonder if you'll ever be able to recover? Tell that to God. Dispense with the polite, positive self-talk and ask God directly, *Where were you when this happened? Were you sleeping? Are you lazy? Are you too chicken and you're hiding?* Take the psalms of lament as your permission slip to be honest with God.

Hatred toward enemies. The second thing we notice when we read the psalms of lament is the way the person who prayed the psalm expressed deep hatred for his enemies. This is what shocked me the most about these psalms when I first read them. Jesus tells us in Matthew 5:44 to love our enemies and pray for those who persecute us. How, then, do we reconcile this command with what we see in the psalms of lament? Look at what a few of the psalmists prayed:

> Arise, O LORD! Deliver me, O my God! Strike all my enemies on the jaw; break the teeth of the wicked (Psalm 3:7).

> Let death take my enemies by surprise; let them go down alive to the grave, for evil finds lodging among them (Psalm 55:15).

> In your unfailing love, silence my enemies; destroy all my foes, for I am your servant (Psalm 143:12).

> O Daughter of Babylon, doomed to destruction, happy is he who repays you for what you have done to us—he who seizes your infants and dashes them against the rocks (Psalm 137:8, 9).

These are a far cry from Jesus' words! I struggled with this for the longest time, trying to reconcile the two differing approaches, and then something happened that seemed to light a path toward clarity.

During church services one Sunday, I taught from the exact passage I quoted above, Matthew 5:44. If you had asked me as I was walking off the stage if the sermon was good, I would have told you that it was probably one of the best sermons I had ever delivered. I was passionate. I drew out the deeper points of the passage and gave inspiring examples of how to love our enemies. I was confident that I had nailed it. Then I walked into the hallway and was greeted by a man who asked me if I had a moment to talk. He pulled me over to the side, made a clenched fist and placed it over his mouth before he said, "Yesterday I pressed charges against a man in our neighborhood for molesting my son. How am I supposed to love that man?"

I didn't know what to say. I stood there speechless. I thought back to my sermon and what it must have sounded like to him, sitting there and listening to me spout off pious platitudes. I hugged that man and prayed with him as forcefully and as passionately as I could.

My sermon had done a disservice to him. It was imbalanced. It wasn't true to what we humans feel when we are wronged. I know that if something like that happened to one of my kids, I would have to be physically restrained from going after the perpetrator. This may not be what you want to hear from a pastor, but it's the truth.

After hearing my friend's story, these two seemingly irreconcilable passages came together for me. Maybe the reason the psalms of lament portray people praying for the destruction of their enemies is because we can't love our enemies until God gives us the ability to love them. And maybe God can't give us the ability to love our enemies until we've expressed to him, in specific detail, the full brunt of our rage and hatred for our enemies. Maybe it's not until we've pulled every last ounce of hatred out of our hearts and flung it onto the lap of God that we can authentically love our enemies. If I had the chance to talk to my friend all over again, I think this is what I would tell him.

Vows of praise. The third thing we notice when we read the psalms of lament is surprising. Interspersed among the kicking, screaming, and pleading is something biblical scholars call "a vow of praise." We see a perfect example of this in Psalm 43, which begins with a desperate petition:

> Vindicate me, O God, and plead my cause against an ungodly nation; rescue me from deceitful and wicked men (v. 1).

But then it ends like this:

> Why are you downcast, O my soul? Why so disturbed within me? Put your hope in God, for I will yet praise him, my Savior and my God (v. 5).

The contrast is so stark, you wonder if the same person is writing the first and the last verses. How can someone go from such desperate circumstances to a position of confidence in God's goodness?

A vow. In just about every psalm of lament, you'll find a statement that expresses, "No matter how dark my circumstances get, no matter how much rage I feel toward God or those around me, no matter how much everything I think and feel tells me to give up on God, I will not. I will not give up on God." Have you ever made a vow like that?

Sister Basilea Schlink, the founder of a Protestant order of nuns in Germany, counsels Christians in the midst of mystery to make a modern day version of a vow of praise:

> When you are in suffering say, "Yes, Father" and strength will flow into your heart.[10]

This is a vow of praise. By making such a vow, we're saying that no matter how alone, abandoned, and betrayed we feel, we will not turn back. By making a vow of praise, we're not forgetting what has happened to us or letting God off the hook. A vow of praise is a declaration in defiance of despair. It is a proclamation to ourselves and those around us.

One of the only ways the saints of old were able to live through unspeakable valleys of desperation was to make vows of praise to their heavenly Father. I want to encourage you to do the same. Don't know where to begin? How about:

Yes, Father, I still believe in your goodness, despite what I see with my eyes;

Yes, Father, I still believe you have a plan for my life, despite what I feel in my heart;

Yes, Father, I still believe my best days are ahead of me, despite what my enemies and friends and family and loved ones say to me;

Even if you ask me to live in mystery the rest of my life, I will wake up every day and say yes, Father, I still believe in you.

OUR FAMILY MYSTERY

I want to end this chapter by introducing you to a
mystery my family and I have been living with as long as I can
remember: my Aunt Lyn. The last time I saw her was last year
at Thanksgiving when our family drove to my parent's home in
Ohio. It usually takes eight hours (and five potty breaks) for our
family to get there from Philadelphia. Thanksgiving with the
Jones clan is a pretty simple affair. The women cook. The men
clean up. Things are much easier that way. We tried it the other
way around once and it wasn't pretty.

Lyn is fifty years old and suffers from schizophrenia. Midway
through the afternoon on Thanksgiving Day, my mom left and
picked her up from the mental facility where she lives. As my
aunt meandered up the driveway, Mom peeked her head inside
the front door and asked if I could help Lyn up the steps. As I
stood up, I looked at my wife with an expression that said, "This
is going to be one more awkward Thanksgiving with my aunt,
just like the rest." I was wrong.

Once Aunt Lyn was settled in the living room, I tried to
make small talk. "What do you get to do where you live?" I asked
without thinking, as if a typical afternoon agenda looked a lot like
a day at summer camp.

"Nothing much. I like going to the cafeteria early. I get extra
ice cream." She giggled. Her laugh can fill an entire room in an
almost embarrassing way. While we sat there, she had moments of
lucidity and I lost sight of her disease. Then without warning, she
cackled again and made a loud irrational comment, and we were
both brought back to reality.

My grandparents have told me that when Lyn was two years old, she tumbled down the basement steps and hit her head. Soon after that she started having seizures, but it wasn't until after high school that Lyn experienced her first psychotic episode and was diagnosed with schizophrenia.

After a few hours that Thanksgiving Day, Aunt Lyn yelled for my mother and then shifted to a child's voice and whispered, "I'd like to go home now." I offered to drive. Her facility was twenty minutes across town. Lyn rode shotgun while Grandma and my mom rode in the back.

On the freeway Lyn laughed and said, "You're a quarterback, aren't you? I can't believe it. I'm sitting next to a cute quarterback!"

"Yep, you got it," I said, "especially the cute part." I hadn't taken a snap from center since I played football in high school, twenty years earlier.

"And you're a preacher too," she said with a serious look on her face.

It was cold in the van. We sat in silence for a few minutes as we waited for the heater to kick in.

"Sing me that song you used to sing to me when we were kids, Darlene," Lyn shouted to my mom.

"What song?"

"You know! That song! I forget how it goes. Sing that one."

"Who sings it?" Grandma asked.

"You know, sing that song you used to sing to me when we were kids," Lyn pressed.

Frustrated, my mom replied, "Lyn, I have no idea what song you're talking about." Then, as if reaching back into some childhood memory, maybe from a bedtime routine, she said, "Lyn, do you mean that Doris Day song?"

"Yeah! Sing me that one. That's it."

My mom started singing, and Lyn immediately joined in, waving her arms back and forth like an orchestra conductor. After a few lines my grandmother chimed in too, and I was struck by the irony of the words:

> When I was just a little girl
> I asked my mother
> What will I be
> Will I be pretty
> Will I be rich
> Here's what she said to me
>
> Que sera, sera
> Whatever will be, will be
> The future's not ours to see
> Que sera, sera
> What will be, will be[11]

My throat started to constrict, and I fought off tears. I couldn't help but see my aunt in that song. In some strange way I think she saw herself in it as well.

As I pulled into the parking lot of her facility, I noticed how much it looked like a regular nursing home. For some reason I had pictured a building at least five stories high with a thick steel elevator and guards posted outside. Aunt Lyn grabbed my arm, and we walked like we were newlyweds. Lyn has a phobia of falling down, so with every bump in the parking lot she slowed down, shuffled her feet, and moaned. Walking arm in arm, with my grandmother behind us, we entered the double doors and were greeted by three nurses sitting at the desk in the hallway.

"This is my nephew, Brian," Lyn said and giggled as she rubbed her head on my shoulder. "I'm in room number twelve, to the left," she whispered in a small girl's voice.

Her room looked like a hospital room. There was a bed with handrails. A sheet divided Lyn's section of the room from that of her catatonic roommate. On the wall my mom had hung a corkboard full of pictures. I couldn't help but notice that I hadn't sent her any. I stared at those pictures and immediately choked up again. "This is her life," I mumbled to myself.

Grandma patted Lyn's bed and tried to act like everything was okay, the way a young mother tries to comfort her three-year-old when dropping her off at preschool. "You walk, you hear. You have to walk. And eat when they take you to the cafeteria." She put her hands on Lyn's shoulders and looked her in the eyes. "You eat what they tell you to eat."

Who dreams their life will turn out this way? I hugged Lyn, promised I would see her soon, put my arm around my grandmother, and we left. We walked fast, faster with every step.

"What are you thinking?" Grandma asked, as if reading my mind.

"I'm thinking you must be a strong person, Grandma."

Back in the van, I tried not to cry. I didn't want to make my mom or my grandmother feel bad, as if I judged them in any way for putting my aunt in that facility. You could hear the sound of the tires hitting the bumps on the freeway the whole way home. I thought back to the song they sang earlier and was angered by the tragedy of Lyn's life.

My aunt missed it all. She never went on a date, attended a prom, or had a boy call her on the phone. She never had her heart race as a man touched her hand and looked into her eyes. She never sat on her knees in her garden as her children played in the backyard and the sun rained down its warmth. I was taken back by the ugliness and pain of it all. Then I cried, silently at first, and then uncontrollably.

It's not fair, I said to myself. *It's just not fair.* I wiped tears away from my cheeks. My mom and grandmother politely ignored my quiet sobbing. They sat and stared straight ahead, taking in the weight of it all. *Where is God in all this?* I kept asking myself. *Did he take one look at my aunt and throw up his hands and say, "Whatever will be, will be?"*

The Bible tells us in Exodus 33:20 that no one can see God's face and live. Before that night I had always assumed that was because God is so holy and powerful that his face is too commanding to behold.

But after that Thanksgiving with my Aunt Lyn, I began to see that passage differently.

Theologians tell us that God is such a compassionate God that his heart breaks for people like my aunt. If what they say is true, then maybe what that passage means is that no one can look at God's *tears* and live.

NOTES

[1]With permission of Liesel M. Tarquini.

[2]Jean-Paul Sartre, translated by Kitty Black, *The Devil and the Good Lord* (New York: Vintage Books, 1960), 140-141.

[3]C. S. Lewis, *A Grief Observed* (New York: HarperCollins, 1994), 44.

[4]Colin Brown, ed., *The New International Dictionary of New Testament Theology* (Grand Rapids: Regency Reference Library, 1986), vol. 3, 501.

[5]See 1 Corinthians 2:7.

[6]See Romans 11:25; 1 Corinthians 15:51; Ephesians 3:6; 5:32; 1 Timothy 3:16.

[7]Eugene H. Peterson, *Under the Predictable Plant* (Grand Rapids: William B. Eerdmans, 1992), 105.

[8]*Webster's New Universal Unabridged Dictionary* (New York: Simon & Schuster, 1983), 1016.

[9]Elie Wiesel, *Night* (New York: Bantam Books, 1989), 60-62.

[10]Sister Basilea Schlink, quoted in Diogenes Allen, *The Traces of God in a Frequently Hostile World* (Boston: Cowley Publications, 1981), 50.

[11]"Que Sera Sera," written by Jay Livingston and Ray Evans, *Doris Day: Greatest Hits* (Sony Music, 1958).

9

Church

The early Christians were not people of standing, but they had a secret power among them, and the secret power resulted from the way in which they were members of one another.

—Elton Trueblood

Over the years I've performed more wedding ceremonies than I can count, but there is one wedding that I am positive I will *never* forget. One morning at our church office, a woman who was not connected to our church knocked on the door and asked if I would be available to officiate at her upcoming wedding. I jokingly call this an inquiry for a "drive-by" wedding because of the way in which a bridal couple flips through the phone book and randomly chooses a church where they'd like to be married; once the ceremony is over they are never seen again.

I typically don't like to do that kind of wedding, but in this situation I had a hard time refusing: the woman's biceps were twice as large as mine! She was six feet tall, with spiked hair and thighs like a professional football player's. She explained that the pastor who was supposed to perform the ceremony had backed out (which should have tipped me off!) with the ceremony just two weeks away. "Please do it," she pleaded. "It's going to be a small ceremony, just friends and family at our house." I felt sorry for her and reluctantly agreed.

When I showed up on the day of the ceremony, I thought I had pulled up to the headquarters of a motorcycle gang. Dozens of "choppers" were parked all over the front yard. Men with long handlebar moustaches wore black leather jackets, jeans covered with leather straps, and German-style helmets with spikes on top. The women riding with them looked like they had been picked up from a Las Vegas showgirl convention. People streamed into the house with cases of beer in one hand and a food dish in the other.

Once inside I was greeted by heavy-metal music blaring in the background and a haze of cigarette smoke. A woman walking by noticed I was the only one wearing a suit and screamed over the music, "YOU MUST BE THE PASTOR. I'M THE BRIDE'S SISTER. TAKE A SEAT IN THE CORNER, AND WE'LL START IN A MOMENT!" As I nodded and hurried over to the corner of the living room to find a chair, I passed a couple passionately making out on the couch. Minutes later the groom arrived with his bachelor-party friends. As the best man stumbled into the chair next to me and passed out, I thought, *Brian, how do you get talked into stuff like this? You see that bulge in that guy's shirt over there? That's a gun, Brian, with real bullets. Do you know what people like this do with guns, Brian? They kill people. That's right, Brian. If you mess up during this ceremony, it's all over!*

Forty minutes and five beers later, the bride's sister called everyone into the living room so the ceremony could begin. A few guys propped the best man up against the wall while someone in the bedroom hit the tape player for the wedding march—an old rock song called "Misty Mountain Hop" by the heavy-metal band Led Zeppelin.

As the bride walked into the room, the guys made noises and hollered to one another. The lace of the wedding dress covered the bride's massive arms but couldn't hide the tattoos from her wrists up to her shoulders. By the time the song ended, she and her fiancé were standing before me with a look of anticipation, so I quickly delivered my typical wedding sermon, pronounced the couple husband and wife, told the groom to kiss his bride, and the place erupted with applause as someone screamed, "Let's party!"

Within seconds everyone in the room swarmed the couple with smiles, hugs, and kisses. My nerves were shot, so I waited my turn in line to congratulate them and offered an excuse as to why I needed to leave. The father of the bride must have overheard me, because he grabbed my arm and yelled to the group, "Let's make a toast!" Someone emerged from the kitchen and started handing out bottles of vodka and wine.

Before anyone could say anything, the bride said, "I want to make a toast myself. I want to toast you guys. You are just like family to me." She looked over at her maid of honor and said, "Jackie, you are just like a sister."

Jackie immediately stopped her and said, "No, you've always been like a sister to *me*." With her arms around the bride's neck, she sobbed, "Do you remember when I lost my baby three years ago? I wouldn't have made it without you." Then she turned to the group and said, "Or without all of you. I wanted to die. You gave me a reason to live."

Arm in arm with Jackie, the bride continued. "Richard, when my brother passed away, you were there for me. You were driving a rig cross-country at the time, but you still came over every weekend."

Someone interrupted her again. "You've been there for us too. When I lost my job, you brought groceries over to my house and bought school clothes for my kids. I'll never forget that. *Never.*"

This went on for more than ten minutes. People shared stories of friends in the group who helped them buy cars when they couldn't get to work. Young mothers explained how other women had watched their children when they were in a pinch. One man told how two guys in the room picked him up from jail and let him live with them until he was able to afford his own place. Despite my initial impressions of these people, I simply couldn't get over the immense love they had for one another. After everyone finished, the bride's eyes panned across the room as she lifted up her beer and said, "To friends." We all held up our glasses and said, "To friends." I looked around the room and thought, *Church should be like this.*

WAYS TO HANG ON

In these last three chapters, we are shifting our focus from why God allows us to go through hard times to three specific things God has provided to help us hang on: the church, ministry, and Heaven. As we begin, I need to acknowledge that most

Christians don't view the church as a place to go when tough times hit. Or perhaps I should say that most Christians who have been followers of Jesus for more than a few years *used* to view the church as a place to go for support when tough times hit. In my experience most Christians become so disappointed with the lack of response to their needs by the church that they stop reaching out. They signed up for Christianity expecting to find authentic, caring relationships like those I witnessed with the group of bikers, but over time they have had to settle for superficial handshakes and "thinking about you" cards.

I'll never forget when a lifelong family friend and mentor tragically lost his son when I was in college. Separated by distance, I assumed that his Christian friends, the staff at his church, and his Sunday school class would step in and wrap arms around him and his wife. I was shocked, one year later, when we were face to face again and I asked how he and his wife were doing. The first words out of his mouth were, "Brian, the church failed us during our greatest time of need." Knowing firsthand his maturity and emotional stability, I was taken back. I couldn't help but think that if he said the church failed them, the church had *really* failed them.

Have you been disappointed by your experience with the church? Do you yearn to be part of something real and life-giving? If so, there is a way to discover or rediscover that. First, I would like to paint as clearly as possible what the church should look like when it is working the way Jesus envisioned. When the community of Jesus' followers is operating the way he dreamed it could work, there's nothing like it in the world. It is truly miraculous. What I saw in the living room at the biker wedding can't even begin to compare with the power and beauty of the church when it is working the way Jesus intended. Then, once you have that picture clearly in mind, I will share a few suggestions for creating this kind of experience in your own church. Just because your church may have disappointed you and your family in the past doesn't mean it has to happen again.

WHAT HAPPENS IN A HEALTHY CHURCH?

People Rally Around Each Other

In his book *Courageous Leadership*, Bill Hybels shares a powerful story about the way people in a healthy-functioning church rally around each other in times of pain.

> I had just finished presenting my weekend message at Willow and I was . . . talking to people. A young married couple approached me, placed a blanketed bundle in my arms, and asked me to pray for their baby.
>
> As I asked what the baby's name was, the mother pulled back the blanket that had covered the infant's face. I felt my knees begin to buckle. I thought I was going to faint. Had the father not steadied me I may well have keeled over. In my arms was the most horribly deformed baby I had ever seen. The whole center of her tiny face was caved in. How she kept breathing I will never know.
>
> All I could say was, "Oh my . . . oh my . . . oh my."
>
> "Her name is Emily," said the mother. "We've been told she has about six weeks to live," added the father. "We would like you to pray that before she dies she will know and feel our love."

Barely able to mouth the words, I whispered, "Let's pray." Together we prayed for Emily. Oh, did we pray. As I handed her back to her parents I asked, "Is there anything we can do for you, any way that we as a church can serve you during this time?"

The father responded with words that still amaze me. He said, "Bill, we're okay. Really we are. We've been in a loving small group for years. Our group members knew that this pregnancy had complications. They were at our house the night we learned the news, and they were at our hospital when Emily was delivered. They helped us absorb the reality of the whole thing. They even cleaned our house and fixed our meals when we brought her home. They pray for us constantly and call us several times every day. They are even helping us plan Emily's funeral."

Just then three other couples stepped forward and surrounded Emily and her parents. "We always attend church together as a group," said one of the group members.

It was a picture I will carry to the grave, a tight-knit huddle of loving brothers and sisters doing their best to soften one of the cruelest blows life can throw. After a group prayer, they all walked up the side aisle toward our lobby. *Where*, I wondered as they left, *would that family be, where would they go, how would they handle this heartbreak, without the church?*[2]

Tucked in the middle of a discussion about the nature of the church, the apostle Paul compared the church to a human body: "If one part suffers, every part suffers with it; if one part is honored, every part rejoices with it" (1 Corinthians 12:26). Paul clearly points out that when we as followers of Jesus become spiritually intimate with one another, it is as if our souls grow together and we begin to share spiritual nerve endings. If something happens to you, I can't help but be affected by it. We are connected soul to soul. In the same way a twisted ankle affects every other part of a human body, the hurt a church member feels touches everyone else in that community. In a healthy-functioning community of Jesus followers, people are deeply connected to one another, and when something happens, good or bad, the instinctive response is to rally around one another.

People Inspire Each Other

The other thing you find in a church that functions the way Jesus intended is regular people inspiring each other by the way they handle the tough circumstances of life. In our church in Ohio, I had the privilege of becoming friends with a man named Bill Clift. Bill isn't a spiritual celebrity. He's never preached before thousands of people or written a best-selling book. He doesn't hobnob with the "who's who" in the Christian community. Bill is a regular guy; a former industrial arts teacher who was forced to go on disability because of a degenerating hip. I never saw Bill walk without a cane, and when he walked his hips wobbled side to side with each step he took. Bill was always the last one to leave our services and hobble out to his car.

Bill had an amazing gift of empathy. When someone in our church went into the hospital to have surgery, Bill would arrive before they arrived, greet the family as they came in, pray with the person about to have surgery, and wait in the waiting room with the family until the surgery was over. Many times I reached the hospital waiting room only to see Bill seated with an entire family standing up around him, holding hands in prayer. It became a joke in our church that people wanted Bill at the hospital with them rather than Pastor Brian. Whenever I picture Bill hobbling around with his cane, I'm reminded of the way theologian Kosuke Koyama described God. Reflecting on his days in the tranquil rice fields of Thailand, he wrote:

> God walks "slowly" because he is love. If he is not love he would have gone much faster. Love has its speed. It is an inner speed. It is a spiritual speed. It is a different kind of speed from the technological speed to which we are accustomed . . . It goes on in the depth of our life, whether we notice or not, whether we are currently hit by storm or not, at three miles an hour. It is the speed we walk and therefore it is the speed the love of God walks.[3]

Bill and God had a lot in common. Bill kept me going through numerous dark days, and that's what I love about the church. When it is working the way Jesus intended, there is always a Bill we can look to for inspiration to keep going. Sometimes it's not enough to have people just rally around you. Sometimes during our darkest moments we need to have real-life people light the way.

Whenever I shared a problem with Bill, he pinched his lips together, looked down at the ground, and shook his head, saying, "Brian, we're just going to have to trust God on this. He'll take care of us. We're just going to have to trust." Trust God? Take care of this? How can this come out of the mouth of a man who, if surgery was an Olympic sport, would always be the gold-medal favorite? Yet, day in and day out, Bill kept going. He never quit or lost faith. Through it all his perseverance kept me going, and I grew to lean on him in ways I'm sure he never ever imagined.

That's what happens in a healthy church: there are always two kinds of people to keep us going. There are the people who rally around us when times get tough and those who inspire us as they walk ahead, clearing the brush and pointing the way. Without either group of people, "church" just isn't the church.

I've been a pastor for a while now, and over the years I've noticed a severe "go it alone" approach among Christians dealing with pain. They will read a book, pray, read the Bible, meditate, journal—all in an attempt to work through their struggles by themselves. All of these things are fine things to do, yet none of them can replace authentic community with other followers of Jesus.

You need the church. You cannot get through what you're trying to get through without linking arms with other followers of Jesus and rallying together. Christianity is not a solo activity. I know you probably have endless reasons why you can't or won't or shouldn't reach out to others in Christian community, but I want to encourage you to ignore those rationalizations. Make a decision right now to step out and seek authentic community with other followers of Jesus. Here's how.

Decide to take a risk. The first step toward living in authentic community with other followers of Jesus is simply making a decision to do so. Years ago I started a bereavement support group for people who had lost family members and friends. Our church had an unusually high number of people grieving the loss of a loved one, so I recruited a wonderful Christian counselor to come and lead an eight-week session. One week after the group was announced, we completely filled up the number of available slots on the sign-up sheet. I was thrilled by the response but also somewhat disappointed, because there was one elderly lady's name not on the list. She and I had become friends, and I knew she was still struggling to let her husband go, even though he had passed away fifteen years earlier.

I called her on the phone and said, "Mary, did you hear that the church is offering a support group for people who have lost loved ones?"

"Yes," she said. "I did."

"Well, would you like to go? The group is full, but I think I can still get you in if you'd like to attend."

"Absolutely not," she said. "I'm not going to go into a room full of strangers and talk about my man," and she hung up the phone. I assumed we had been disconnected, so I called her right back and said, "Mary, this is Brian again, I was wondering if—" *Click.* She had hung up again.

I shouted into the phone, "Crazy old woman!" and dialed her number again. "Mary, this is—" *Click.*

I couldn't believe it. I dialed her again. "Mar—" *Click.*

I tried once more. She didn't even bother talking this time; she just picked up the phone as soon as it rang and hung it up again.

That Sunday Mary smiled at me and said, "I'm sorry, Brian. I just can't. I can't bring myself to do it. I hope you understand."

Two weeks later the group started with a room full of hurting people. Women who were grieving miscarriages joined the group. One woman had lost her sister in an airplane crash. My friend Philip from chapter three was there; Claire had gone home to be with Jesus. The group grew so close that they didn't want to disband after eight weeks. They kept going. Two people who met in the group actually ended up getting married. It was an amazing experience. Yet I always felt a twinge of sadness whenever I thought about that group because my friend Mary missed out. The group could have changed her life if she had just given it a chance.

Don't make the same mistake my friend Mary made—make a decision to take a risk. C. S. Lewis once said in his masterful book *The Four Loves:*

> Love anything, and your heart will certainly be wrung and possibly be broken. If you want to make sure of keeping it intact, you must give your heart to no one, not even to an animal. Wrap it carefully round with hobbies and little luxuries; avoid all entanglements; lock it up safe in the casket or coffin of your selfishness. But in that casket—safe, dark, motionless, airless— it will change. It will not be broken; it will become unbreakable, impenetrable, irredeemable.[4]

Don't let this happen to you. Make the decision right now that you're going to step out and risk living in Christian community.

Start small. My grandmother was born in 1923 and grew up during the Great Depression. She told me that during that difficult time, people wandered door to door with their children, asking for food scraps. People quickly found out that my grandmother's parents were generous people. Anyone who came to the door received food if there was any to give. After a while so many people were coming to their house that they wondered how news of their generosity had spread. One day my great-grandfather inquired, and he was told, "Because of the *X*." On the side of the house, someone had scratched a large *X* that signaled to people walking by that this house was a place you could get your needs met. My advice to you is the same: find some people in your church and mark each other with an *X*. Look each other in the eye and say, "We're going to live in community with one another. We don't know exactly what that looks like right now, but we're making a commitment today to live as followers of Jesus *together* and find out." This could be a small group, a class, a ministry team, or simply two or three friends with a similar interest. How it starts and how it is organized isn't as important as why it exists.

The purpose for your group should be pretty simple: to obey everything Jesus commanded, together. Jesus said in Matthew 28:20 that the whole goal of being his followers is to obey his teachings, so that's your mission. Figure out how to obey them together, in your neighborhood, in the twenty-first century, with your own combination of personality types, genders, interests, gifts, and backgrounds. Meet as frequently as you can. Try to humbly live out the Christian faith, one day at a time. I know it seems like it should be much more complicated than that, but it really isn't. Christian community is nothing more than inviting Jesus to be in the center of our relationships and spending time with one another worshipping God and reading, discussing, praying about, and obeying Jesus' teachings. That's Christian community.

As you stick with it, over time you'll discover something amazing. Your experience will go beyond simple friendships and fun outings to sharing things you never dreamed you'd share with another living person. You'll find yourself taking risks you never dreamed you would take. Fears will be challenged. Sins will be confronted. Tears, healing, and forgiveness will become your constant companions, and it's all because Jesus promised in Matthew 18:20, "Where two or three come together in my name, there am I with them." Live in his presence. Do what he commanded. Obey his teachings. Love God. Love people. Be authentic. Hold nothing back. Over time you'll never want to leave each other's presence.

A few years ago another pastor and I traveled to Orlando to attend a church conference. One afternoon we had a break, so we decided to take a "field trip" to Disney World and experience the park from a leadership perspective, asking ourselves what makes the park "the happiest place on earth" as Disney parks are known. We interviewed anyone who would talk to us and learned unforgettable lessons. The signage was amazing. The attention to detail was spectacular. Everything was done to create "just the perfect moment" for people from all over the world. But the thing that stuck with me the most was what happened in the parking lot as we arrived. Boarding the tram, I noticed a car in the distance with all four doors open wide and security guards rummaging through it. I leaned over to the tram driver and said, "Terrorists?"

"No, tourists," he replied. "They left their car running, doors wide open, and ran for the entrance."

I said, "That has to be the most hysterical thing I've ever heard. Has it ever happened before?"

He looked at me over his shoulder and said, "About five or six times a day!"

Over the years I've been to Disney World a few times, and I've been in a few groups committed to living out Jesus' message. I have to say that my initial excitement for Disney blew away my initial interest in being a part of my groups. When we first met in homes or at the church, it was more than a little awkward. It took time to get to know one another and to trust each other. We had to navigate through the initial stages of personality conflicts and power struggles. We had to say good-bye to a few people who found out they really weren't interested in doing life Jesus' way. Yet over time, as we stuck with it, a simple mystery began to unfold: Jesus showed up.

On occasion we'd sense his presence, and then it would be gone. Over time, the deeper we shared, the harder we prayed, and the more we encouraged each other to obey, the more he seemed to leave his footprints in the carpet of the room. Those times together created a thirst unlike anything I had ever experienced. On those days I had to make sure I turned my car off and shut my car doors; I was that excited about being together with my friends. The only difference between those times and the few times I walked onto Main Street, U.S.A.® in Orlando was that my experience with my Christian friends was real. Yours will be too, if you take a risk and start small.

Stick to one church. Besides taking a risk and jumping into community with other followers of Jesus, there is one more thing you must do to make authentic Christian community happen: you have to stick to one church for the long haul. After church services one Sunday, a couple greeted me on their way out the door. By their cliché Christian lingo, I knew they weren't our typical nonreligious visitors. "Pastor, what an anointed word from God you delivered today," the husband said. I cringed. Normally the only people that talk that way are on really scary Christian television programs. I swallowed and said, "Hope to see you next week."

His wife looked at me with a grin and said, "Nope. We won't be back. Years ago the Lord told us to attend a different church every week. So we'll be somewhere else next Sunday."

I said, "Let me get this straight. You go to a different church every week?"

"Yep," said her husband. "Been doing it for five years now."

I said, "How sad."

"Why do you say that?"

"Because you never get a chance to experience real Christian community," I replied. "You're, like, connoisseurs of fine churches. My hunch is it wasn't the Lord who called you to do this. Find a church and put down roots."

We've become a nation of church shoppers, and unfortunately this couple wasn't far from the norm. If the preaching gets boring at our church, we pull out the yellow pages. If the worship style changes, we go to First Church's early service. If our Sunday school class starts to get too impersonal, we don't sweat it; we try the hot new church in town. We Christians change churches like we change favorite restaurants. I can't help but think this must make God sad.

In the New Testament there are dozens and dozens of things Christians are told to do. Leaving one another is *not* one of them. In fact, we're told to do the exact opposite.

Is there someone at your church you can't stand? First John 3:11 tells us to "Love one another."

Did the pastor at your fellowship hurt your feelings? Colossians 3:13 says, "Forgive whatever grievances you may have against one another."

Do the attitudes of the people in your church family need to change? James 5:16 says, "Pray for each other."

In other words, roll up your sleeves and do the hard work of building community where you are. Don't go spiritually AWOL. Stick it out, through exciting times and boring times. Pray, serve, love, forgive, sacrifice, and resolve like authentic followers of Jesus. Christian community isn't something that happens instantaneously. Real community is forged on the anvils of time and struggle. If you jump ship when things get tough, you'll condemn yourself to one long journey of spiritual superficiality.

I know this from experience. My parents started attending Eastpointe Christian Church in Columbus, Ohio, when they were both teenagers. They're now in their sixties. They've never joined another church. Over the past fifty years, they've seen quite a lot. They lived through the "clapping in church" controversy of 1976 as well as the mediocre church softball team of the early 1990s. They've seen people get married, have children, and those children get married and have children. They've seen hundreds of people come to Christ and some of those people fall by the wayside. They've buried dear friends. They've served with great pastors and mediocre pastors and experienced great worship and boring worship. Through calm years and tumultuous years, my parents have given, served, and prayed their entire lives in that one church.

One day in the future, both my mom and dad will pass away, but right before that happens they'll each be able to do something someone who has spent a whole life church shopping cannot—they'll look back and savor the memories a lifetime of faithful participation in one congregation brings. They'll look back and relish the dangerous conversations they didn't avoid, sins they were encouraged to confront, and authentic Christian friendships it took a lifetime to develop. Jesus wants you to experience the same thing.

I'm sure you know this already, but it's worth repeating: That "perfect church" you're looking for already exists. You attended it last Sunday.

NOTES

[1]Elton Trueblood, *The Yoke of Christ* (Waco: Word Books, 1975), 25-26.

[2]Bill Hybels, *Courageous Leadership* (Grand Rapids: Zondervan, 2002), 22-23.

[3]Kosuke Koyama, quoted in Tony Lane, *The Lion Concise Book of Christian Thought* (Oxford: Lion Hudson, 1984), 225-226.

[4]C. S. Lewis, *The Four Loves* (New York: Harcourt, 1988), 121.

10

Ministry

The extreme greatness of Christianity lies in the fact that it does not seek a supernatural remedy for suffering, but a supernatural use for it.

—Simone Weil

I'll never forget where Tattoo Man lived: corner apartment, right-hand side, directly in front of the broken-down Chevy El Camino. He made quite an impression the first day I met him as I made my way down the line of apartments, handing out food and praying for people. I knocked on his door and waited forever. Eventually I heard his gruff smoker's voice: "Yeah, what do you want?"

"I want to show you God's love in a practical way. Do you happen to need some groceries and prayer?" With lightning speed he opened the door, snatched the bag of groceries, and slammed the door. "Okay!" I shouted. "We'll pray next time."

Two weeks later the same thing happened. When I knocked on his door, he grabbed the food so fast I didn't even get a look at his face. I snapped my fingers and said, "Got me again!" The next time, however, I was much quicker. As soon as he lunged for the groceries, I stepped back and said, "Why don't I pray for you first?"

He slowly walked outside. He was wearing nothing but a pair of shorts, and he was covered with tattoos, from the top of his head to the bottom of his feet. I'm not talking about a few tattoos here and there—every inch of his body was covered with them, hence the nickname.

"You want to do what?" he asked.

"I'd like to pray for you. Is there anything that's weighing on your heart?"

He stretched and yawned and said, "Man, its early . . . um . . . I don't know . . . uh . . . how 'bout my son? That's it. Pray for my son. He's in a track meet today. Pray that he makes me proud."

I placed my hand on Tattoo Man's shoulder and prayed that God would help his son run to the best of his ability and bring him and his dad closer together. Without saying a word, he grabbed the groceries and slammed the door behind him. I walked away and said, "That's a start."

A few weeks later when I approached Tattoo Man's apartment again, he didn't wait for me to knock. He ran outside and said, "Religious Guy, never thought you'd come by again. My son, you know the one you prayed for, he made it to the sectionals! I need you to pull down some favors with, you know, the *Big Man*."

I said, "Let's see what we can do." Placing my hand on his shoulder, I prayed again. As soon as I finished, he picked up the groceries, gave me a thumbs up, smiled, and walked inside—a big improvement from any previous visit.

The next time, Tattoo Man was waiting for me outside on the porch. "The regionals!" he yelled. "He's going to the regionals! I'm so stoked! Let's pray again."

I sat down next to him and said, "How about you? I'd like to pray for you first. If Jesus were sitting right here, what would you ask him for?"

He looked down at the ground and mumbled, "I'd ask him to help me get off cocaine and get a job. I have to get out of this place. I'd ask him to help me be there for my kids. I want to make my son proud."

When I knocked on his door a few weeks later, Tattoo Man yelled, "He's in the state championship today! Right now to be exact. Mile relay. He's gonna win. I can feel it."

As I stood there listening to him brag about his son, I couldn't help but picture a young kid on one of the biggest days of his life, looking up at an empty bleacher seat where his father should have been. Had I known Tattoo Man wasn't going to be at that track meet, I would have taken him myself, but it was too late. I was so sad and frustrated by the whole situation that I couldn't even pray. I just reached over and hugged my friend, reminding him of his prayer to make his son proud.

Soon afterwards Tattoo Man disappeared. I didn't hear from him for quite some time.

But two years later, at a different apartment complex, I turned a corner and a huge man bumped right into me. I looked up and said, "Tattoo Man?"

"Door-knocking Pastor Guy!?" he screamed, and picked me off the ground and shook me up and down so hard I almost passed out.

I couldn't believe it. I said, "How in the world are you doing? I lost track of you."

"Yeah, I went down a bad road," he said, "but God worked a miracle. Look at me. I've got a job doing maintenance at this apartment complex. I met a wonderful Christian woman, started attending church, and last year I became a Christian. Best of all I'm completely clean from cocaine, and I'm a real dad again. You started it all. Thank you."

I felt an incredible swell of pride, the way I feel when one of my daughters sings at a school concert or scores a goal in a soccer game. I put my hand on his shoulder, looked him in the eye and said, "I knew you could do it. I just knew it."

This all happened at Parkside Homes, the housing project I described in chapter four. I was so excited about what happened with Tattoo Man that I made a last-minute change to my Sunday sermon. I told my church Tattoo Man's story and taught on Galatians 6:9: "Let us not become weary in doing good, for at the proper time we will reap a harvest if we do not give up."

After the sermon a friend of mine had a question. "I don't get it," she said. "That's a nice story and everything, but the guy didn't end up coming to our church. I don't get why you keep doing that kind of stuff." It was a sincere question on her part.

I hesitated, looked her in the eyes, and said, "Honestly, it never even crossed my mind whether he would come to our church or another church. I just wanted to help him find Jesus and—"

She cut me off. "Yeah, but why do you keep *doing* these things? These people will never come to our church."

"You mean extending them compassion and introducing them to Jesus?" I shrugged my shoulders. "I guess all I can say is that for some reason I need to do this *for me*. I know that sounds selfish, but it's the truth."

BREAKING THROUGH DESPAIR

In John Bunyan's classic allegory of the Christian life, *The Pilgrim's Progress,* the central character, Christian, flees the City of Destruction and seeks eternal life. During his long pilgrimage he walks on the narrow path of the Hill of Difficulty, down through the Valley of Humiliation, passes through the Valley of the Shadow of Death, and eventually reaches the Celestial City. Along the way he meets the characters Mr. Worldly Wiseman, Hopeful, and Faithful. At one point on his journey, Christian narrowly escapes the Doubting Castle, which is guarded by the Giant Despair. Thinking that those following behind him might fall into the giant's lethal grip, he decides to make a sign to warn future sojourners about the giant. The sign he erected read:

> Over this stile is the way to *Doubting Castle;* which is kept by Giant *Despair,* who despiseth the King of the *Celestial Country,* and seeks to destroy his holy pilgrims.

Then Bunyan adds:

> Many, therefore, that followed after, read what was written, and escaped the danger.[2]

I must not have been paying attention while I was pastoring in Ohio, because I blew right past that sign. During that time my soul was in the grip of the giant. I was miserable beyond description. I was angry, bitter, depressed. I slept too much, ate too much, and withdrew from people. I stopped smiling. This was one pilgrim the giant had no problem overpowering. Then something happened: the more I reached out to people like Tattoo Man, the more wiggle room I noticed in the giant's grip. Over time, while throwing myself into the lives of other people, serving them, and loving them, both in our church and at places like Parkside, each act of love and service brought me a little closer to home.

Do you find yourself in the lethal grasp of despair right now? God has provided a second way for you to hold on during life's difficult moments. In addition to living in authentic Christian community, serve others. As you serve others in the midst of your pain, orienting your entire mind, heart, and soul around serving others in Jesus' name, four things will happen that will loosen the giant's grip on your soul.

SHIFTING THE FOCUS

When I was a kid, our backyard was a young boy's wonderland, filled with oak trees that seemed to touch the sky and visited by squirrels, rabbits, and the occasional deer. During the fall so many leaves fell on the ground that we could rake them into piles eight feet high and jump into them off the roof. There was a downside to all the trees, though—the poison ivy that wrapped around their trunks in late spring. One day in the fourth or fifth grade, I chased a baseball behind a tree, and sure enough, one day later poison ivy covered my arms and hands. My mom put some medication on it and sent me off to bed. The next morning I woke up to discover that I had scratched the poison ivy so much during the night that it had spread all over my face and ears.

I was miserable. It itched so much I could barely stand to stay in my own skin. That night my mom rubbed more medicine on me and warned that if I continued scratching, the poison ivy would continue to spread. But I couldn't stop, and I woke up the following morning looking like a poison ivy zombie. In desperation I devised a solution that was foolproof. Each night before I went to bed, I put on winter gloves and taped my hands together with duct tape! Within a week the poison ivy blisters disappeared.

My method of treating poison ivy illustrates one way we should approach our emotional wounds in times of pain—leave them alone and resist the urge to keep meddling with them. It sounds counterintuitive, but it works. When we feel physical pain in our bodies, our natural response is to ice, massage, set, bandage, or medicate until it gets better. If it continues to hurt, we obsess over it until the pain goes away. In Matthew 16:25, however, Jesus gives us insight into one of the ways we should deal with our emotional pain: "Whoever wants to save his life will lose it, but whoever loses his life for me will find it."

The word Jesus uses for "life" in this verse is the Greek word *psyche,* which is the Greek word for "soul."[3] The soul, according to Jesus, has its own way of making itself better, but it also has its own way of becoming toxic. Ultimately, the health of the soul is dependent upon the way we orient our lives. We become spiritually sick when, like incessantly scratching our poison ivy, we become obsessed with our own pain. Often we'll buy every tape and book we can find on the subject and spend endless years making personal healing our sole pursuit in life. As long as the pain is the least bit present, we don't care how long it takes to make the pain go away—we're not leaving our own bedside until we've made a full recovery.

According to Jesus, one of the ways soul wounds heal is by leaving them alone and focusing the energy we're tempted to expend on them outside ourselves instead. I do not want to imply that seeking counseling, acquiring medical treatment, setting clear personal boundaries, or taking care of ourselves emotionally and physically are wrong. I believe these activities can be an important part of "losing our lives." Learning to give up our demand for everyone else to make us happy and taking responsibility for our own lives is extremely important. But even these positive activities can be taken to the extreme if we're not careful.

That's why balancing self-care with serving is so important: it takes the focus off me in a natural way. It breaks me out of any possibility of self-obsession, no matter how well intended. Notice how one second-century Christian document called *The Didache*, which means "The Teaching," began its instruction to new Christians. The very first line reads, "There are two Ways: a Way of Life and a Way of Death, and the difference between these two Ways is great."[4]

Are you hurting? Do you feel like you can't break out of the giant's grip? Choose the path that leads to life. Ignore what your intuition tells you and break outside yourself in order to serve others in spite of your pain. Heal your wounds by focusing your energy elsewhere. Trust Jesus' instruction that as we focus on others we find our souls again. I do not doubt that I became so miserable during the difficult time in Ohio because I did the exact opposite of what I should have done—at the first sign of pain I focused inward and began to brood. My internal negativity began to feed on itself, and my soul shrank a little bit more every day. It wasn't until I began to take the focus off myself that I was able to allow my soul the space and time to heal.

Don't do what I did. Find someone to serve. Serve Christians. Serve non-Christians. Find your life by losing your life in others. In doing so you'll find that your own pain grows smaller and smaller each day.

AWAKENING EMOTION

The second thing serving others does for us is give us an opportunity to *feel*. When we're in the giant's grip, it can seem as if we're inside an emotionless bubble, as though a thin strip of plastic insulates our soul's emotional sensors from everything we touch. Things that used to make us cry or make us mad no longer do so. All emotions—sadness, happiness, rage, empathy, and passion, especially passion—elude us at every turn.

Jane Kenyon describes what it is like emotionally to be in the grip of the giant. In her poem "Pardon" she writes:

> A piece of burned meat
> wears my clothes, speaks
> in my voice, dispatches obligations
> haltingly, or not at all.
> It is tired of trying
> to be stouthearted, tired
> beyond measure.
>
> We move on to the monoamine
> oxidase inhibitors. Day and night
> I feel as if I had drunk six cups
> of coffee, but the pain stops

abruptly. With the wonder
and bitterness of someone pardoned
for a crime she did not commit
I come back to marriage and friends,
to pink fringed hollyhocks; come back
to my desk, books, and chair.[5]

One day during my period of despair in Ohio, I became tired of being stouthearted, so I grabbed the keys off my desk and drove to a nursing home around the corner from our church office. I didn't know anyone there. I just knew that I was tired beyond measure and figured the best way to reconnect to my soul was to serve others. I walked into the foyer and a nurse asked, "Family?"

"No," I said, "discouraged pastor." She smiled and said, "Feel free to encourage yourself by visiting anyone you'd like." I had four hours, so I made it my goal to visit every resident.

As I walked into room 144, I found a man lying motionless on his bed. By the bedsores on his arms and legs, I could tell he had been in that position for a very long time. I sat down and said, "My name is Brian, and I'm a pastor in the area. I wanted to come by to keep you company and to see if there is anything you'd like me to pray for." No response. His eyes didn't even move. I wondered if he could even hear me. I wondered if his mind was so far gone that I was wasting my time. I didn't know what else to do, so I gently placed my hand in his and prayed. I had no passion or intensity; I just forced myself to do it.

I prayed that he would feel God's presence in his heart, even though I wasn't feeling it myself. I prayed that his time left here on earth would be full of love. I prayed that he would come to know the love of Jesus before he left this life. I prayed all kinds of things that I wished were true for me, but weren't. Then as I finished and pulled my hand away, the man startled me. He grabbed my hand and wouldn't let me go. For the first time he looked over at me. I tried to pull my hand away again, but he squeezed it that much harder. I wasn't sure what to do, so I just sat back in my seat and waited. For ten minutes we sat there, silently staring into each other's eyes.

To be honest, at first I felt a little odd. I imagined family members walking in behind me wondering who this nut was holding the hand of their loved one. Then I let go, not of his hand, but of my pretense and inhibition. I looked into his eyes and tried to imagine what Jesus saw. Eventually, as I sat there caressing his hand, my new friend gently closed his eyes and fell asleep.

Years later I still look back on those moments in that room with a sense of wonder. I had walked into the room emotionally void, but when I left I took something away with me—a feeling, a reminder, I can't describe it accurately—but it was tangible. I *felt* something, as surely as I am breathing. Whatever it was, it was a gift, and that gift gave me the strength I needed to keep going.

Some people will try to discount your emotions when you are going through a dark stretch. You might hear things like, "You can't trust your emotions. Your faith should be based on fact, not feeling. Don't place too much stock in your emotions." You can thank these people for their advice but quickly set it to the side. What I felt that day in that nursing home saved my soul. That man's gift to me was incalculable. The story may seem small or petty, but when the world has gone gray and the soul has gone numb, small may be all we've got. Yet it can be enough to kick-start your journey home.

Around the year AD 125, Christians were being severely persecuted and even murdered for their faith. To turn the tide of public opinion, a gifted Christian writer named Aristides crafted a detailed defense of Christianity and delivered it to the Roman emperor Hadrian. Look at how Aristides described the selfless way Christians served people in Jesus' name:

> They love one another, and from widows they do not turn away their esteem; and they deliver the orphan from him who treats him harshly. And he, who has, gives to him who has not, without boasting. And when they see a stranger, they take him in to their homes and rejoice over him as a very brother; . . . and if there is among them any that is poor and needy, and if they have no spare food, they fast two or three days in order to supply to the needy their lack of food.[6]

If you feel, as Jane Kenyon wrote, like a piece of burned meat has stepped into your clothes, I'd like to encourage you to take the next two months and dedicate yourself to mimicking those second-century Christians. Find a widow, buy her groceries, and clean her house for two months. Visit an orphanage and volunteer to tutor the children. Find a homeless person and bring him or her into your house. Get her job training. Help him find transitional housing. Homeless people are no more or less dangerous in the twenty-first century than they were in the second. Fast for two or three days and take the money you would normally spend at the grocery and give it to someone who is without food or resources. Do this for a few months and you'll feel something inside yourself you thought you'd never feel again: hope.

EXPERIENCING GOD'S PRESENCE

One of the hardest things about that dark period in Ohio was the way proven spiritual practices completely broke down for me. When I prayed, I felt nothing. When I read the Bible, it might as well have been Tolstoy's *War and Peace*. Everything seemed flat. This really worried me, not so much that I couldn't connect with God but that my tried-and-true methods for connecting with him had fallen apart. Initially I appreciated the value of divine silence, but after a while I grew fearful. I continually wondered at the time, "God, why can't I *feel* you?"

Then something completely unrelated happened: businesses in the area of our church office started complaining about the area saloon. Years before I moved to town, a local businessman had opened an old-fashioned drinking- and pool-playing saloon. This wasn't your trendy twenty-something socialite nightclub. People got in fights at this place. Beer bottles were left in the parking lot, and the police were frequently called late at night. Over time a groundswell of support to oust the saloon mounted. Even though our church was not involved in the complaints, I feared that the saloon's owners and employees would assume we were responsible because our church office was located just a few hundred yards away. I felt I needed to do something, not so much to show them our support, but to show them a simple act of Christian love.

I was sharing my concern with a friend from the church when suddenly I had an idea. "I've got it. Let's clean their toilets!"

My friend looked at me and said, "Dude, are you nuts?"

"Come along and let's find out." We grabbed two buckets and

all the church's cleaning supplies, walked down to the saloon, and opened the front door. I spotted a bartender at the counter and introduced myself. "We're from the church down the street and wanted to know if we could clean your restrooms."

"Is this one of those hidden-camera TV shows?" the bartender asked.

I assured him it wasn't. Then I explained that we were aware of the current backlash against the saloon from others in the community and that we just wanted to show them God's love. He pointed to the restrooms and said, "Knock yourself out."

Have you ever been in the restroom of a saloon? Not the cleanest place in the world! Hair, bottles, and vomit covered the floor. I took the toilets and my friend took the floor and sink. As we scrubbed the place down, the saloon employees opened the door to see what we were doing and yelled back to their buddies, "You weren't kidding. I can't believe it!" The smell of the place almost made me vomit. Human feces were caked all over the toilet and on the walls. I felt bad for my friend; I had talked him into coming, but he served as joyously as if he were singing on our worship team. An hour and a half later, when we were finished, we walked out into the bar drenched in sweat and thanked the bartender for the opportunity to serve.

I didn't realize it at the time, but that ninety-minute germ-fest brought me closer to God than an entire week's worth of praying and reading the Bible. Serving touched my soul in a way prayer, Bible study, and worship had not been able to do at that time. I found so much spiritual refreshment in the simple act of serving that I made a decision to go back to the saloon as often as I could and serve those people in Jesus' name until God helped me break free from the giant's grip. At the time I was pretty sure I was the only pastor who conducted his devotional time in the restroom of a saloon.

To this day, sometimes the only way I touch the hem of Jesus' garment is by serving others. I know this will sound sacrilegious, but the most important advice I can give you, if you are having trouble hanging on, is this: if you can't pray, stop trying to pray. Gather all your devotional books and prayer journals and throw them into a box. Run away from churches advertising sermons on prayer and all of the other neat, American, utilitarian approaches to connecting to God. Give yourself permission to connect with God in another fashion. If it lasts a week, so be it. If it lasts three months, so be it. Enter into a season of serving and listening and be perfectly content with that. As Oswald Chambers said in his spiritual classic *My Utmost for His Highest,* "Are you in the dark just now in your circumstances, or in your life with God? Then remain quiet. If you open your mouth in the dark, you will talk in the wrong mood: darkness is the time to listen."[7]

FINDING MEANING IN SUFFERING

The final thing serving others does for us is keep us from wasting our pain. The first time I used that phrase, I was sitting across from a man who had just divorced his second wife. She had verbally abused his two daughters from the time they were eleven until he left her. "I knew I should have gotten out earlier," he said, "but I kept holding out hope. One day she would be fine and the next day she'd snap. I'll recover from this, but my daughters— I put them through hell. I don't know if they'll ever forgive me, and if they do, what kind of scars will they carry?"

I sat for a long time listening to the man's story, trying to offer as much support as I could. Two hours into our lunch, he looked at me and asked, "What lesson does God want me to take from this?"

Without even thinking I said, "Don't waste your pain."

The question we need to ask ourselves when God allows us to go through hard times is not why but who? In the mind of God, pain always has two intended recipients: us and someone else. If we choose not to take what we've experienced and find some way of using it to help other people, we miss a large part of why God allowed us to suffer in the first place.

In his book *The Gospel of Suffering,* philosopher Søren Kierkegaard asked:

> When indeed does the temporal suffering oppress a man most terribly? Is it not when it seems to him that it has no significance, that it neither secures nor gains anything for him? Is it not when the suffering, as the impatient man expresses it, is without meaning or purpose?[8]

Absolutely. Suffering is pointless when it is without meaning, and suffering is without meaning, ultimately, when what we've suffered isn't put to some greater use. Let your mind wander for a moment and think of ways God might want to use what you've suffered to help serve other people in Jesus' name.

• Maybe you've struggled with infertility. How could God use what you've learned through that struggle to help other couples facing the same circumstances?

• Maybe you were abused as a child. Could God be nudging you to write poetry, magazine articles, or books to help others?

• Maybe you've struggled with unemployment. Does your church have a ministry poised to help similar people in your community? Could you help start one?

• Maybe you've had a bad accident and still feel its effects. How could God take your pain and turn it into a blessing for other people?

I taught a Bible study one night on the subject of abortion. Even though I tried my best to be as gracious and sensitive as possible, a woman in the group came up to me afterward visibly distraught. As a teenager in high school, she had been talked into having an abortion by her controlling boyfriend and regretted it immensely. I pointed her to a crisis pregnancy center, and she quickly became their lead volunteer counselor. She could have chosen to conceal her pain, like so many women in her situation do, and silently live with her wounds the rest of her life. Instead, she chose to give herself and her story away. I couldn't have been more proud of her. She didn't waste her pain, and whatever you do, please, don't waste yours either.

Just before we moved from Ohio to Philadelphia, the church we had planted had grown enough to need to raise money to build our own permanent building. Two years earlier I honestly didn't think we were going to survive. Instead, by God's grace, we began to grow, and over time the church flourished and became a beautiful community of Jesus' followers. Along the way we added staff, bought eleven acres of land, and were ready to impact the community in an even greater way. The only thing that stood in the way was money for a new building.

With the help of an outside consultant, we decided to run a fund-raising campaign that would end with a large banquet where financial pledges would be collected and announced. Committees were formed. Flyers were distributed. I preached for weeks about stewardship and how this building would enable us to reach more people with the message of Jesus. Commitment forms were passed out. The atmosphere in our church was euphoric.

The banquet was held in one of the nicest hotels in Dayton. Everyone dressed up. The meal was catered, and the worship team from a sister congregation came and sang. It was quite an event.

I had instructed the ushers to seat any latecomers to the banquet at my table, but I was surprised when a man our church had helped move off the streets walked into the banquet hall with his *entire* halfway house. Of course he was welcome, but I thought maybe he had misunderstood the purpose of the meeting. In the announcements that morning, had he heard the phrase "free meal" and stopped listening after that?

The group was a sight to behold. The former homeless man, Pete, was wearing a suit jacket, but his pants were ripped and stained. His tie was bunched around his neck in a knot. Pete was flanked by his girlfriend who, when she laughed, cackled so loudly that everyone in the banquet hall turned and looked. When she smiled, you could see the food lodged in between her teeth. To Pete's left was another friend, who sat down and said, "I'm glad Pete told us about this free meal." (I thought to myself, *This meal's not free!*)

At first I was a little perturbed by the lack of return on investment represented at my table at this fund-raising event, but as the evening continued my mood went from slightly embarrassed to inspired. Every time an announcement was made, my table, the halfway house gang, cheered wildly. Pete would scream, "Oh yeah!" and pump his arms up and down. His friends would go around the table and high-five one another. My wife and I just laughed.

At the end of the evening, the campaign chairman came forward and said, "This is the moment we've all worked toward these last four months. Inside this envelope are our campaign commitments!" I happened to look over at Pete, who was bouncing in his seat the way a five-year-old does when he is seconds away from being handed a present he's wanted for months. For some reason, right at that moment, instead of turning my eyes back toward the campaign chairman, I kept staring at Pete. The envelope was opened, the commitment total was announced, and in what seemed like slow motion, Pete shot out of his chair and screamed with everyone else in the room, "We did it! We did it! We did it!"

I was immediately mobbed by other people in the congregation, who were all ecstatic. I got up and hugged everyone on the committee, the speaker, and anyone else I saw. After the celebration calmed, Pete wiped a tear out of the corner of his eye, laid a huge bear hug on me, and said, "We did it, big guy. We did it. I just knew we'd do it."

That's when it hit me.

The reason God had moved my family to Ohio to start a new church was more than that building. Maybe all the pain of the early years of planting that church—all the heartache, all the discouragement, all the days I yelled out to God and begged him to let me quit—maybe all of that had a point to it. Maybe God had a reason behind everything that happened to me those first two years, and maybe that reason was standing right in front of me.

NOTES

[1]Simone Weil, translated by Arthur Wills, *Gravity and Grace* (New York: G. P. Putnam's Sons, 1952), 132.

[2]John Bunyan, *The Pilgrim's Progress* (New York: The Heritage Press, 1942), 137.

[3]Colin Brown, ed., *The New International Dictionary of New Testament Theology* (Grand Rapids: Regency Reference Library, 1986), vol. 3, 676.

[4]"The Didache" in *Early Christian Writings* (New York, NY: Viking Penguin, Inc., 1987), 191.

[5]Jane Kenyon, "Having it Out with Melancholy" in *Constance: Poems* (St. Paul: Graywolf Press, 1997), 24.

[6]*The Apology of Aristides*, translated from the Syriac version by D. M. Kay, chapter XV. http://www.earlychristianwritings.com/text/aristides-kay.html.

[7]Oswald Chambers, *My Utmost for His Highest* (New York: Dodd, Mead & Company, 1935), 45.

[8]Søren Kierkegaard, translated by David F. Swenson and Lillian Marvin Swenson, *The Gospel of Suffering* (Minneapolis: Augsburg, 1948), 126-127.

11

Heaven

*I divested myself of despair
and fear when I came here.*

—Jane Kenyon

The first theological question that I couldn't answer didn't come from a renowned theologian at Princeton Seminary or even from an atheist I was trying to convert. It came from the mouth of a freckled-faced seventh-grader in a junior high Sunday school class. At the beginning of a lesson about eternal life, I asked the class, "What do you think Heaven will be like?"

Dead silence. I knew half the class was still asleep, but I had sixty minutes to go, so I persisted. "Come on, guys, I can't do all the taking here. What do you think? What will Heaven be like?"

Dead silence again. I had exactly three weeks of junior high Sunday school teaching under my belt, so I knew what to do.

I looked at the kid yawning the loudest, squinted my eyes like a high school biology teacher about to ask a profound question, and said in my most reverent voice, "Josh, let us begin with you. What do you think Heaven will be like?"

Josh looked at me and said, "I think it will be *stupid.*"

I blinked. I couldn't believe it. I leaned forward and said, "Stupid? You've got to be kidding me. How can Heaven be stupid?"

He shot back, "It sounds stupid. I don't want to go there."

I said, "Yes, you do!"

He said, "No, I don't."

"Yes, you do."

"No, I don't."

"Yes, you do."

"NO, I DON'T!"

"YES, YOU DO!"

"Read my lips: N-O-I-D-O-N-apostrophe T."

I knew I shouldn't throw my Bible at my Sunday school students, so I took a deep breath, counted to ten, and asked, "Josh, I'm curious. Why don't you want to go to Heaven? Don't you want to be with Jesus?" The entire class was wide awake now.

The girl sitting next to Josh laughed and said, "Yeah, Josh. You don't want to go to Hell, do you?"

I held up my hand and said, "Hold on. Nobody's going to Hell here."

"Well, Josh is *definitely* going to Hell," she said. "Don't you go to Hell if you don't go to Heaven?"

I cut her off, turned to Josh, and said, "Why don't you share with us what you're thinking."

Then he did it. He asked the question. Only five words in

all, but profound enough to show the rest of the class that I was clueless: "What makes Heaven so great?"

WHAT MAKES HEAVEN SO GREAT?

As I fumbled around for a fitting response, the students sitting there that morning saw right through me. Everyone knew that Josh had stumped the teacher. It wasn't that I didn't know most of the correct theological answers; I just hadn't lived long enough to believe them myself. There was no longing in my voice to show my students that I looked forward to going to Heaven. After my bumbling response, Heaven appeared a lot like Josh had described it.

That was twenty years ago; a lot has happened since then. Until that day I had experienced very little sadness in my life, but since then I've taken one long detour through what philosopher Miguel de Unamuno called the "tragic sense of life."[2] My life since that day, while both beautiful and stark, has given me a little more perspective from which to approach Josh's question. So I'm going to take a "do over" and take one more shot at answering it.

No Joint Custody

In an effort to discredit Jesus in front of his followers, a group of religious teachers called the Sadducees asked him a question which seemed to have no clear answer: "If a woman gets married and her husband dies, and then she marries again, and that new husband dies, and this continues seven different times, who will be her husband in Heaven?" (Luke 20:27-40). Everyone stared at Jesus. He looked at the crowd and answered,

"The people of this age marry and are given in marriage. But those who are considered worthy of taking part in that age and in the resurrection from the dead will neither marry nor be given in marriage" (vv. 34, 35). This insightful response caused the Sadducees, who did not believe in life after death, to back off and leave Jesus and his followers alone.

Jesus' answer is often heard as a *promise,* even though it was not intended to be. Why? People read that passage and think, *In Heaven, I won't have to endure the painful effects of my parents' divorce any longer.* For them, their parents' divorce ranks as *the* most painful experience in their life, and the possibility that there might be another world where relationships do not disintegrate before their eyes seems too good to be true, but it isn't. In Heaven, kids never have to hear the words, "Your mother and I are getting a divorce." Second-graders are never forced to choose sides in court. Ten-year-olds don't spend every other weekend at their dad's house or have to meet their mom's new "friends." In Heaven, people neither marry nor are given in marriage, and for many people that is Heaven enough.

No Racism

Another thing that makes Heaven so great is the way people will interact with each other. When I entered junior high, I quickly established two goals for my seventh-grade year: get Kacey Gire to kiss me and keep my friend Eric Green and me out of the hospital. Every morning as Eric and I walked to Rosemore Junior High School, we had to pass a gang of guys that called themselves "The Cornered Rats." They were big and scary, did drugs, and most mornings they outnumbered us fifteen to two. I had the misfortune of being an athlete who lived in a nice house. Eric had the unfortunate problem of being an athlete and black. Some days we ran. Some days we fought. Most days we came home terrified. Not a single day went by in all of seventh grade when my friend Eric wasn't called a "nigger." At the end of the school year, Eric and his mom moved to Cincinnati so he could attend a more racially mixed school.

Revelation 5:9 gives us a glimpse into what Heaven looks like. Speaking to Jesus inside the throne room of Heaven, the angels cry out:

> You are worthy to take the scroll
> and to open its seals,
> because you were slain,
> and with your blood you purchased men for God
> from every tribe and language and people and nation.

What a beautiful image. Because of Jesus' death on the cross, Native Americans in Heaven stand next to whites, Hispanics next to Koreans, and Italians next to blacks. People are no longer divided by customs or language as they are here on earth, but joined together as one family, the people of God. In Heaven best friends never move because their mothers are scared they'll end up in the hospital because of the color of their skin. Seventh-grade boys never run home with dislocated jaws, bleeding knees, torn clothes, and the nickname "nigger lover." Racial slurs don't enter anyone's mind in Heaven. No one wanders onto a showroom floor, receives bad service, and later wonders if it was due to her ethnicity. Fear is gone. Hatred never enters our minds. Reconciliation and forgiveness flow like spring-fed streams. In Heaven everyone is treated the same, at all times, in all places, by all people.

Children Are Never Molested

A thirteen-year-old boy from a church I served walked home from school one day, and instead of turning right, he turned left and walked straight into the local police station. His exact words to the man at the desk were, "My father has been molesting me for as long as I can remember. Can you make him stop?" Children never have to make left-hand turns in Heaven.

No Handicapped Signs

On July 24, 2000, I told a bold-faced lie. Our family was at Walt Disney World's Epcot Center for a vacation, and after paying for our tickets we were told by a security guard that we wouldn't be allowed to bring our baby stroller inside. The temperature that day was ninety-nine degrees; our youngest daughter was only eight months old but weighed nearly thirty pounds, and carrying her around all day in the sweltering heat seemed unthinkable. The security officer said that if we went to the main security pavilion we might be able to get a special exemption, so I wheeled her to the office and went inside.

"Sir," a woman told me, "we cannot give you a permit to use your stroller inside the park."

I countered, "I wish you would have told us that before we purchased our nonrefundable tickets. There's no way I can carry her around all day."

Then she asked, "Does she have a special medical condition? If so, I can give you a permit that you can put on her stroller that will allow you to enter each ride and exhibit through the handicapped access."

I paused. Wheels started turning. I was desperate. I was

stupid. I was sweaty. I anticipated needing back surgery after the long drive home. I looked outside at my daughters jumping up and down, waiting to go inside, and then I did it: I leaned over and said, "Uh, she's got FBS syndrome."

"Well, why didn't you mention that when you came in?"

"It's rare," I told her. "I don't like drawing attention to it."

She scribbled "FBS syndrome" on a little yellow tag and handed it to me. "Place this on your stroller handle and show it to the operator of each ride and exhibit. They'll let you right in."

I thanked her and walked out the door, knowing full well that I was headed straight toward the pit of Hell. I showed my wife the yellow tag. "What's FBS syndrome?" she asked.

I whispered in her ear, "Fat baby syndrome."

Lisa laughed, "She's not fat!"

"Have you held her lately?" I said.

The rest of the day, despite the protest of my wife, we used the stroller and rode every ride and walked through every exhibit. The only problem was having to use the handicapped access. As the day unfolded, I began to wonder if God wasn't using my lie to teach me a greater lesson.

At first I thought it was funny that we were able to bypass hour-long lines and walk straight to the front of a ride. Then I started to notice the people with whom we were spending time: mentally challenged children in wheelchairs, adults with cerebral palsy, kids on ventilators. I'll never forget the image of one young boy who needed three Epcot workers just to help load his wheelchair onto a ramp. His head gently lay to the side on a headrest, and his arms were strapped to the wheelchair with large black bands. Behind his back sat a large computer that regulated his breathing. His parents and two brothers walked slowly at his side, adjusting his breathing tube as the Epcot employees gently maneuvered his wheelchair onto the ride.

That day marked me. For twelve long hours, ride after ride after ride, I was given a front-row-seat view of the painful lives of the physically broken. For the people at Epcot that day, Heaven will be a day of liberation. There are no ventilators in Heaven, no handicapped access ramps, no beds with rails. No one needs someone else to bathe them, feed them, push their wheelchair, write for them, or hold the phone up to their ear. In 1 Corinthians 15:42, 43, God promises a new beginning for them all. "The body that is sown is perishable, it is raised imperishable; it is sown in dishonor, it is raised in glory; it is sown in weakness, it is raised in power." What an amazing day that will be.

Kids Don't Watch Their Parents Die

When I was in the fifth grade, my Uncle Bob died of a heart attack while shoveling snow in his driveway. He was thirty-nine years old. I can still picture my cousin Debbie at his funeral: arms crossed and a look of defiance on her face, head and chest shaking with sobs, looking straight ahead like it was all a cruel game. Twelve-year-old girls shouldn't have to put their entire world in a box and bury it in the ground. Seventeen-year-old girls shouldn't have their mothers meet their prom dates at the door. Twenty-five-year-old women shouldn't have their uncle walk them down the aisle on their wedding day. Thirty-four-year-old women shouldn't have to say to their children, "Your grandpa would have loved seeing you play soccer today."

Revelation 21:4 tells us that in Heaven kids never attend their parent's funerals. It promises, "He will wipe every tear from their eyes. There will be no more death or mourning or crying or pain, for the old order of things has passed away."

People Don't Hurt Each Other

A friend and his wife went on a date and left their thirteen-month-old son with a teenage babysitter. When they came home, the child was sound asleep, but in the morning his mother found him lying on his bed having seizures. They rushed him to the hospital where doctors ran tests and concluded he had suffered severe trauma to the head, leaving him with permanent brain damage. My friend was told that it looked like someone had grabbed his son by the shoulders and shaken him back and forth like a rag doll. He now wears what looks like a football helmet wherever he goes. He can't walk. He can't see. He can't talk. My friend and his wife drive two hours, three times a week, just to take him to a specialist. The babysitter was never convicted. Another thing that makes Heaven such a wonderful place is that people don't hurt each other there.

Newborns Never Die

Years ago on a cross-country trip to the Grand Tetons and Yellowstone, our family stopped for the afternoon in Salt Lake City, the headquarters of The Church of Jesus Christ of Latter-Day Saints, also known as the Mormons. We toyed with the idea of going out to the Great Salt Lake and floating in the salt water, but because of time constraints chose instead to spend the day touring a small area downtown called the Temple Square. Surrounded by high walls and wrought-iron gates, the Temple Square is home to the beautiful Mormon Temple and other awe-inspiring buildings. Near the end of the day, I saw a building with a sign that read "Family History Library" and asked a tour guide what was inside. He said, "That's the home of the greatest genealogical library in the world. People come from all over the planet to search for their ancestors at that library."

I always had an interest in tracing my family history, so I looked at Lisa and said, "We're doing it." We walked inside, asked a volunteer for instructions, sat down at a computer terminal, and started typing family names into the search engine. I entered my father's name and came up empty handed. I entered my grandfather's name and the search found nothing as well. Then I entered my great-grandfather's name, and the computer's hard drive began making noises and pages and pages of information filled the screen. Confused, I caught the attention of the volunteer in our section and asked, "What does all this mean?"

She answered, "Someone belonging to the LDS church has traced your family line." She leaned over my shoulder and said, "Let's see here. It appears that your family line ends at AD 1020. Someone traced your family line back nearly a thousand years."

I felt like I was in Atlantic City and had just won a million dollars on the nickel slots. I raised my hands in the air and shouted, "Oh yeah, baby! I'm awesome at this!" Then I leaned over to my wife, who was shaking her head and rolling her eyes, and I said, "These Mormons don't know who they're dealing with. I'm a one-man genealogy machine!"

This experience sparked a new hobby. After vacation I began collecting every story, picture, birth certificate, and marriage license I could locate. Eventually I hit a dead end at four generations of Joneses and decided I would visit my great-aunt Pauline, one of my oldest living relatives at the time, to see if she had any interesting family stories to share. One morning I packed our family into our minivan and drove from Dayton, Ohio, to Pikeville, Kentucky, to see if Pauline could fill in any of the gaps in our family history.

On the way to her nursing home, I stopped at an old Jones family cemetery someone had told me was located on top of a small mountain in Harold, Kentucky. The cemetery was small, just a few gravestones in all, but eerily placed among them were four small markers that all read "Baby Jones." Each marker had dates showing how long the babies lived, ranging from just a few days to a little less than a month. Lisa looked at me and said, "How sad. Whose babies are these?"

"I don't know," I said. "We can ask Pauline."

After lunch we drove on to the Mountain Manor Nursing Home where my aunt was living at the time. We hugged her, sat down next to her bed, and told her we were in town for the day to find out more about our family history. We talked about her declining health, her son Bobby who was a schoolteacher in the area, and how everyone in our family loves University of Kentucky basketball. Eventually I turned our discussion to our family tree and mentioned to Pauline we had visited the old Jones family cemetery up the road. I told her about the four small markers we had noticed and asked whose babies they were.

Without hesitating she said, "They're mine. I buried those babies myself, every single one of them."

"Did you have miscarriages?" I asked.

"No," she said. "I carried them each to full term. They died afterward." Lisa reached over, grabbed her arm, and said, "I'm so sorry, Pauline. "That must have been awful." Pauline nodded and turned her head toward the window and stared outside. A single tear slowly rolled down her cheek. It was clear my question had burrowed into a sacred, pain-filled place in her past.

People in Heaven never have to smooth the dirt over a child's grave. Words like Sudden Infant Death Syndrome and Rh factor are never used. No one ever sees a woman carrying post-pregnancy weight but not a child and asks, "Oh, are you expecting?"

Over the past two decades I've seen so much brokenness, I could continue on for pages more. In Heaven family members don't discover the bodies of loved ones who have committed suicide. No one dies in automobile accidents, on operating tables, or from old age. There are no strange food allergies, people shed their mental illnesses like old coats before they go there, and there's never any need to take sleeping pills. Memories of mistakes we made as parents don't haunt us anymore. No one is considered ugly. There's no minimum wage, no wars or terrorists or military budgets, no tsunamis, earthquakes, hurricanes, or tornados. There's no such thing as an addiction, and no need to leave flowers on anyone's grave. Tumors can't ravage our bodies in Heaven, and no one steps across homeless people while getting on the bus.

I could go on and on. Yet, as great as all of these things are, there is one more joy of Heaven that outshines them all.

We're Finally Home

I have a recurring dream. The first time I had it, after the death of my grandfather, I thought it was special but of no real consequence. Since then I've had the exact same dream the night after the funeral of every Christian loved one in my family. This dream's effect on me has been so powerful that in a way I now look forward to having it.

Whenever a Christian family member passes away, that evening in my sleep I return to the backyard where I grew up. I see the huge oak trees in the yard and a large picnic table on our patio. Each time I have the dream, the table gets larger. There's a picnic taking place. On the table is a neatly placed red and white checkered tablecloth. In the center of the table are large buckets of chicken surrounded by baked beans, potato salad, corn on the cob, and coleslaw. I'm always standing inside my house, peering out the glass door like I'm spying on someone. As I'm standing there, the person whose funeral I just attended that day slowly walks in from the right.

As the person appears, I always see my grandfather look up and smile. He never smiled a lot when he was alive, but he's smiling in the dream. He stands up, wipes his hands on a napkin, and reaches out and kisses the new person at the table on each cheek. People stand up, laugh, and greet one another like they had been expecting each other. My grandmother is the last one to join them at the table. She is wearing a white blouse and blue pants. Her tightly-permed hair looks just like she always had her hairdresser style it while she was alive, once a week, every week. Now, however, she's walking upright. Her face looks much younger. The weathered lines on her face are gone. She's laughing. She's not wearing dentures, so the first thing she grabs is an ear of corn.

In my dream as I stand in the house watching this, I always feel like I'm trying to cry, my throat knotting up in a ball. It's a strange sensation. As the dream brings me back to all of these people who have touched my life in such profound ways, I am overcome with feelings and memories I haven't experienced in years. With each dream the feelings become more intense. Each time I'm taken back to the picnic, I want to stay there a little longer. I want to talk to everyone. I try to push the door open and tell them that I'm there, but each time I do so, I wake up. I get angry and try to force myself back to sleep, but once I'm awake the dream is gone, until next time.

This longing and feeling of connection with these people only strengthens and grows because of something else I always see in the dream. It's always a light, a sort of center of warmth, or presence. Just outside my vision to the left, blocked by the door, something is sitting, or rather, someone. At first I didn't know who it was, but each time I'm taken back to that place, the more certain I become about who is sitting there. I can't see him, but I see his presence reflected in the people sitting at that table. I can see his attributes bouncing off their faces. No matter how hard I might squint and maneuver my body, I never see him, but each time I'm there I feel him in the same way, just like I feel the sunshine on my face on a warm summer day.

I know the dream isn't real, but somehow I don't think the dream is the point—the point is the longing that induces the dream. My desire for something that endures beyond the grave is real. The yearning, the hope for something beyond this life, never leaves. It only intensifies with time. The dream, in my mind, is only a reminder of something that stirs much deeper inside me. C. S. Lewis called it "the secret signature of each soul, the incommunicable and unappeasable want."[3] The neurons in my brain are only reaching for the most potent memories, images, and emotions it can grasp to remind me, if only a few times in my lifetime, that something exists beyond this world, a place, a dimension—I don't have the words to describe it, but it's real. Everything within me knows this place exists. The Bible calls it Heaven. To me it simply feels like home.

Throughout this book we've spent a great deal of time talking about all the possible reasons why God has allowed us to suffer and how we can hang on during those difficult times. One day very soon all of that won't matter any longer. One day, the chemo drips will end, the nights spent wondering where God is leading you next will come to a close, and all of the anxiety you've felt worrying about your son or daughter will evaporate before your very eyes. On that day your need for answers will fade into the background as you notice someone walking toward you on the faint horizon. Shrouded in light, you'll barely be able to make out the silhouette. But as each step brings him closer toward you, you'll begin to feel a sense of certainty, a weightlessness you've never felt before, the brief pain of expectation in your chest. This longing, a feeling you've but touched as it grazed your soul during your time on earth, this presence will be standing right before your very eyes. Jesus will smile, hold out his arms, and suddenly all the pain and suffering you've endured in this life will be lost in his grasp as he utters the words you've been longing to hear: "Welcome home. Welcome home."

NOTES

[1]Jane Kenyon, "Notes from the Other Side," *Constance: Poems* (St. Paul: Graywolf Press, 1993), 59.

[2]Miguel de Unamuno, translated by J. E. Crawford Flitch, *Tragic Sense of Life* (New York: Dover Publications, 1954).

[3]C. S. Lewis, *The Problem of Pain* (New York: HarperCollins, 1996), 150-151.

ACKNOWLEDGEMENTS

I want to thank the wonderful people at Standard Publishing for taking a risk on the message of this book. Bruce, Diane, Lindsay, Lynn, and Dave—it has been a privilege serving Jesus with you.

The following communities of faith have been an incredible source of encouragement in my life. Whether I ate graham crackers in your nursery or was the pastor of your church, you all have kept me pointed in the right direction as I stumbled along toward the cross: Eastpointe Christian Church, Reynoldsburg, OH; Fairfield Christian Church, Lancaster, OH; Sherbourne Christian Church, Sherbourne, KY; Tilton Christian Church, Tilton, KY; LifeSpring Christian Church, Cincinnati, OH; Newtown Christian Church, Newtown, PA; Levittown Christian Church, Levittown, PA; Princeton Community Church, Princeton, NJ; First Christian Church, Clearwater, FL; Northern Hills Christian Church, Clayton, OH; Christ's Church of the Valley, Collegeville, PA.

Five dear friends, much smarter than I, agreed to read and critique each chapter as it was finished. They were an invaluable sounding board for me as I committed ideas to paper. For their investment of time and friendship, I would like to thank Liesel Tarquini, Jessica Miller, Diane Karchner, Jeanne Lasko, and Gail Bunning.

My church allowed me three months to do nothing except speak on the weekends and write this book. Without my friends, colleagues, and partners on staff at Christ's Church of the Valley covering all the bases in my virtual absence, this book would not have been possible. I don't think I could love and respect another group of people as much as I do Frank Chiapperino, Terri Stone, Carrie Silver, Janet Flitter, Robin Feick, Stephanie Carter, Leanne Stolpe, Lisa Jones, Mary Archey, Matt Silver, Leland Sapp, Ben Foulke, Janine MacGregor, Lisa Bergman, and Kevin Stone.

While everyone on staff read and commented on chapters of the book, special thanks goes out to interns Emily Mace and Melissa Jaworksi for locating publishers' addresses for quotation permissions, and to Lisa Bergman, who tirelessly ran down quote citations, proofed chapters, and performed a million other tasks so I could focus on the message of this book; I simply could not have written this without her support. Extra special thanks goes to Kevin Stone, my friend and our executive pastor, who kept the CCV ship headed in the right direction while I wrote. It is because of his positive attitude and unending sacrifice that I was able to stay glued to my laptop.

To my sisters, Sherri and Laura, who are just as shocked as I am that their brother turned out to be a Christian, let alone a writer, I offer my thanks as well. Though separated by many miles, serving Jesus in different parts of the country, you are never far from my heart and mind.

My mom and dad, Charles and Darlene Jones, were the first and greatest spiritual influences in my life. Anything I accomplish of any worth to the kingdom can be placed solely at their feet. My mom was the first one to believe me when I told people I became a Christian, the first one to think it wasn't absurd that I wanted to become a pastor, and the first one who didn't think I was crazy to turn my scribbling into a book. My dad is the greatest spiritual leader I have ever been around. Wherever I am, regardless of the situation, if I don't know what to do I always find myself asking, *What would my dad do here?*

My daughters, Kelsey, Chandler, and Camryn, are the joys of my life. Watching them grow up, seeing their faith blossom, and being by their side as they take risks, explore the world, and emerge into beautiful women like their mother has been one of the greatest honors of my life.

Finally, little did I know when I saw that cute little girl with the big brown eyes playing tetherball with a friend at Round Lake Christian Assembly that she would become my future wife, lover, and best friend. My wife, Lisa, as W. H. Auden said, is "my North, my South, my East and West." It is with my deepest affection that I acknowledge her encouragement and participation in the ministry of this book.

—Brian Jones

For more information about the author's writing, visit his website, www.brianjones.com.

RENOVATE YOUR LIFE

Let *Trading Places* help you make a change that will last forever. Courage alone won't sustain lasting change. True life change is a renovation only God can pull off, and He wants to pull it off — in partnership with you.

STEVE WYATT
TRADING PLACES
ALLOWING GOD TO RENOVATE YOUR LIFE

0-7847-1840-7

"*Steve Wyatt writes with the authenticity of someone who has lived every word. Be warned in advance: This book may leave you in a different place than it found you.*"

—Gene Appel, Lead Pastor, Willow Creek Community Church